CHAPTER 1
STARTING OVER

O N NOVEMBER 7, 1972, a relatively unknown lawyer named Joe Biden pulled off a big political upset. By just over three thousand votes, he defeated the two-term U.S. Senator J. Caleb Boggs. At twenty-nine, Biden became the sixth youngest senator in U.S. history.

Despite his narrow and amazing victory, Biden almost didn't take the oath of office. On December 18, 1972, just five weeks after his huge election victory, Biden headed to Washington D.C. to interview possible staff members. At home in Delaware, his wife, Neilia, took their three children shopping for a Christmas tree. While running their errand, a tractor trailer slammed into the family car, instantly killing Neilia and their one-year-old daughter, Naomi. Biden's four-year-old son, Beau, and three-year-old son, Hunter, were critically injured.[3]

In the weeks following the death of his wife

and daughter, Biden was an emotional mess. He described the feeling of losing his wife and daughter as a "hollow core" that grew inside his chest like a big black hole.[4] Though he never contemplated suicide, he suddenly understood how it seemed like a rational option to those who were in the depths of despair.[5] There were also feelings of anger. Lots of them. Unable to find comfort in his Catholic faith, Biden would walk the streets of Wilmington at night, hoping to get in a fight so he could take his rage and worry out on someone else.[6] Despite these feelings, he tried his best to focus on his surviving boys and "putting one foot in front of the other" so he wouldn't be swallowed by that dark abyss.[7] His future in the United States Senate, something he had worked so hard for, suddenly didn't seem that important. Speaking to the Democratic National Convention in 2008, Beau recalled his father saying, "Delaware can get another senator, but my boys can't get another father."[8]

Biden was faced with a critical choice that would define the rest of his life: resign before taking the oath of office, or do the job the people of Delaware elected him to do. Life as a senator was a busy one. To be successful, it required a lot of energy—something Biden no longer had. Resigning most likely meant returning to practicing law. The latter wasn't a bad option, but it wasn't the one that Biden really wanted. Politics still interested him, even though his passion had been temporarily put on hold.

Eventually, with the urging of other senators and the thought that getting elected was something for which he and Neilia had worked too hard just to give up, Biden agreed to give his Senate career six months, planning to resign once that time passed. In January of 1973, Biden took the oath of office at his sons' hospital bedside. Because he still wanted to be there for his sons as they recovered from their injuries, he gave up the home he and his late wife were planning to buy in Washington D.C. and commuted to and from his home in Delaware—a practice he continued as long as he served in the Senate.

Life wasn't easy for the young senator. Like most widowers, Biden struggled to make it through one day at a time. Initially, he did the least amount of work required for his job. He cast votes when needed, but avoided building relationships with other senators and didn't work to get certain bills pushed through committee. "My future was telescoped into the effort of putting one foot in front of the other," Biden wrote. "The horizon faded from my view. Washington, politics, the Senate had no hold on me... I could not bear to imagine the scene without Neilia ..."[9]

One of the things Biden did consider, though, was relocating to Vermont. [10] It would be a perfect way to start over. No one would know anything about him, his two sons, or their tragic loss. He and his boys could begin a new life and put the loss of his wife and daughter behind them. Senate staffers started taking bets on how long Biden would last at his job.[11]

But as the months passed, Biden grew tired of grieving. Though he still felt that big black hole inside him, he started taking his job as a senator more seriously and becoming involved in the actual day-to-day work of the Senate. He arranged for his sister, Val, to care for his sons while he commuted to work. His six-month self-imposed deadline arrived without him noticing.[12] For the next two years, Biden did the best he could, dividing his time between Washington D.C. and his home in Delaware.

As he began putting the pieces of his life back together, Biden started thinking about dating again. In March 1975, he noticed a series of ads in an airport with an attractive blonde model. Biden thought it would be nice to meet that woman.[13] Just a few days later, he got that chance. One of his friends gave Biden the phone number of a woman he thought Biden would like. As it turned out, the woman happened to be the same model he had seen in the airport photographs. Her name was Jill Jacobs. Biden was smitten with her on their first date. When Biden went home later that night, it was the happiest he'd been in two years.[14] He couldn't keep Jill out of his mind. Jill, however, was less than enthusiastic about getting involved in a serious relationship. She was recently divorced and was finally enjoying being single again.[15] Besides, Biden was ten years older than her, and dating someone involved in politics, especially a senator, was something she had no real interest in.

Biden was determined and didn't let her objections stop him from pursuing her. Slowly, their relationship became more serious. As Biden fell more in love with Jill, the shattered pieces of his life started to come together. His interest in life and politics was renewed. For the first time since Neilia died, Biden felt like he could be himself again.[16] Biden attacked his role as a senator with renewed vigor. He worked hard to make connections and build the relationships he needed to be influential and successful at his job.

Despite the progress Biden was making, Jill was still very hesitant to get married. She was about to start a job in the fall as a teacher and was unsure about becoming a mother to two young boys. Biden asked Jill to marry him. She said no. He asked her three more times. She turned him down again and again and again. Finally, exasperated, Biden told her he loved her too much to just be friends. She finally accepted his offer and they were married on June 17, 1977—four-and-a-half years after the death of Biden's late wife.

Biden was well aware of Jill's feelings about politics and told her he wouldn't run for re-election in 1978 if it meant making her happy. At home one day, they discussed his future. Biden picked up the phone and dialed a reporter at the *Wilmington News-Journal* to tell him he wasn't running for re-election. As the phone rang on the other end, Jill took the phone from him, hung it up, and told him not to make the call. Later she told Biden, "If I denied you your dream, I would not be marrying the man I fell in love with."[17]

Biden ran for re-election, won with fifty-eight percent of the vote, and continued what was to become a successful political career. He was re-elected five more times to the U.S. Senate. In 2008, after a second failed attempt to become the Democrat's presidential nominee, Barack Obama asked Biden to be his vice presidential running mate. During his acceptance speech at the 2008 Democratic National Convention, Biden said something that summed up his life and career: "Failure at some point in your life is inevitable, but giving up is unforgivable."[18]

***

It wasn't just luck that brought Joe Biden and Jill Jacobs together. Before they met, Biden made three important decisions that readied him to date and eventually remarry. Jill already had many concerns about getting serious with him, and had Biden made different choices before they met, their relationship might not have lasted very long. Biden wasn't thinking about dating or having a new relationship when he made these decisions. Even so, they helped him build a foundation better prepared him to date and eventually marry Jill.

CHOICE #1: BIDEN KEPT HIMSELF BUSY

Biden's first important decision came weeks after Neilia's death: He had to decide whether or not to be a senator. No one would have blamed Biden for quitting the Senate after losing half his family. He could have easily returned to Delaware and quietly continued his law practice. He could have folded, stayed at home, and let the anger and the big black hole in his heart consume him. Instead, Biden chose to work. At first, he did so half-heartedly, doing just the minimal amount of work to get by, but his job gave him a routine and something to help pass the time and distract him from his loss.

Keeping busy is important after loss. Whether it's a job, hobbies, or other busywork, it's important to have something else to focus on. Though it doesn't matter what you do, it does help if what you're doing is something you are passionate about. Work gives you a routine and a reason to get out of bed in the morning. Those with nothing to do focus on their grief and sink deeper into sorrow and despair, which is bad for their physical health, state of mind, and overall quality of life. It also makes it difficult to date when you're sad and thinking only of yourself.

After the loss of my wife and daughter, my job was about the only thing that got me out of bed in the morning. Like Biden, I did the minimal amount of work necessary. I'd show up, do what was required, and leave as soon as I'd put in the necessary hours. I didn't socialize with coworkers or attend work parties or other events. I got in and got out and did it five days a week. I didn't love my job, but looking back, it was good that I had something to distract me for eight hours a day.

If you don't have a job to go to, find a worthy cause and volunteer your time. There are plenty of charitable, religious, civic, and political organizations that are looking for people to help move their cause forward. Find one that you care about and see what you can do to help. Keeping busy will do wonders for your state of mind and help return some meaning and purpose to your life.

CHOICE #2: BIDEN CHOSE TO BE A FATHER TO HIS SONS

Biden had two young boys who were both seriously injured in the accident. They needed a father. Biden knew that being a senator would be a time-consuming job. His sister, Val, and her husband moved in to help care for the boys while he was away at work, but Biden knew his boys were worried that he would leave for work, get in some sort of accident, and not come home. Biden made it his priority to come home every night, eat dinner with them, and talk to them before they went to bed.[19] He did this even if it meant turning down invitations to parties and other social functions most senators attended after the Senate's business was concluded for the day.

Biden also gave his boys the right to talk to him at any time for any reason. It didn't matter who he was meeting with or what he was doing—Biden told his staff to put his boys through whenever they called.[20] When car phones became available, he had one installed in his car so he could talk to them on the way to and from work.[21] Finally, he gave his boys the permission to come to work with him whenever they wanted. All they had to do was let him know they wanted to come, and he would take them to the office.[22]

Being a single father is hard. Combine the duties of a single dad with the loss of a spouse, and it can make a difficult task nearly impossible. Biden, however, did everything he could to be a father to Beau and Hunter. That meant supporting the family, enforcing house rules, and trying his best to give them a semblance of normal life. And when he realized he couldn't do it alone, he reached out to his sister and asked for help. Juggling work life and home life wasn't easy for Biden, but it would pay dividends years later when he introduced his sons to Jill and they started a new life together.

It's easy for widowed parents to think only of themselves and neglect their duties and responsibilities as a parent. Sometimes they'll give their kids too much freedom while they deal with their own issues. They may stop enforcing house rules, stop expecting their children to get good grades, and start excusing bad behavior because the kids are grieving. However, Biden's commitment to his children wasn't just a way to help his children adjust and heal—it was also a way to help mend himself.[23]

CHOICE #3: BIDEN EMBRACED HIS NEW LIFE

Eventually Biden realized that being holed up in his office thinking about his late wife and daughter all the time wasn't doing him any good. He started putting more time and effort in to his job. As a result, his self-imposed six-month deadline to give up his job as a senator came and went without him noticing.[24] He stopped thinking about moving far away and started living the life he had. He also stopped being angry at God and realized that there were many other people in the world who had problems and challenges that made his look small in comparison. Biden still had his health, a Senate seat, and two boys he could go home to every night. To remind himself of what he still had, Biden kept a cartoon on his desk of someone who just suffered bad fortune shaking his fist at God and asking, "Why me!?!" To which God replied, "Why not you?"[25]

Rather than giving up, he adjusted to life as a widower and single father and worked to overcome the challenges that were thrown in his way. In addition to becoming more involved in his job, he also went on the occasional date.[26] There were still plenty of difficult days ahead, but they became fewer and farther between the more he started living his life and accepting his new reality. By the time Biden met Jill, he had reached a point where he was more than ready to open his heart to someone else and begin a new chapter of his life.

STARTING OVER IS A CHOICE

In the weeks and months following the death of his wife and daughter, Biden defined himself by his loss. He was a widower: nothing more, nothing less. Eventually, he started thinking of himself as a father and a senator. With the support of family, friends, and Senate colleagues, he was able to take the shattered pieces of his life and build a new one. It's not hard to imagine Biden's life taking a different direction if he had let the anger, despair, or sadness get the best of him.

In order to date successfully again, you need to reach a point where you identify yourself as something other than a widower. This isn't something that just happens. It's the result of choices you make before you even think about dating. It involves laying the groundwork and being mentally and emotionally ready for the possibility of opening your heart to another woman. Reaching this point takes a lot of time, patience, and work. It involves navigating an emotional minefield as well as dealing with children, friends, family, and former in-laws who are still grieving the death of a mother, daughter, and friend. It takes the mental fortitude to pick yourself up from the ground (or get out of bed) after a bad day. There are going to be lots of setbacks and adjustments. There will be days where all the effort you're making is for nothing.

But once you've laid a foundation, when you find that special someone, things will fall into place. Suddenly your life will be full of laughter and joy, and you will find yourself glad to be alive. And because of all the grief, the pain, and the setbacks you've endured, you will relish and cherish those moments of joy and happiness like you've never cherished anything in your life. Suddenly that missing energy, passion, and zest for life that left when your wife died will return with a vengeance.

Successfully starting a new chapter in your life doesn't require falling in love again or tying the knot a second time. It doesn't even involve dating again, unless dating is something you want to do. Starting over involves making the necessary mental adjustments in order to deal with life without your spouse by your side. It involves making a conscious decision to be happy and move forward even on days when it takes every ounce of strength just to get out of bed in the morning. But for most widowers, having the chance to open their heart and love someone just as intently as before is what gives them the passion and spark to embrace work, hobbies, and life with renewed vigor.

If you're thinking about dating again or have already started dating, keep reading. Dating is an entirely new adventure the second time you try it.

CHAPTER 2
HOW SOON SHOULD WIDOWERS WAIT BEFORE DATING AGAIN?

T HOMAS EDISON'S MOTHER, Nancy, passed away on April 9, 1871, at the age of forty-three. Edison's father, Samuel, wasn't content to live life alone. A mere three weeks after his wife's death, he started a relationship with the family's sixteen-year-old housekeeper, Mary Sharlow. [27] Samuel was six-ty-seven. There is some debate as to whether or not the couple actually married or had a common-law relationship, but whatever their marital status, their relationship horrified their neighbors and the residents of Port Huron, Michigan. They were "the brunt of myopic, small-town gossip" during their life together. [28] Despite their fifty-one-year age difference, the couple had three daughters and stayed together for more than twenty years—until Samuel's death in 1896.

Thomas Edison apparently had no issues with

his father's actions. If anything, his father's second marriage may have gotten Edison finally thinking about his own love life. That fall, the twenty-four-year-old Edison started dating sixteen-year-old Mary Stilwell—an entry-level employee of his News Reporting Telegraph Company.[29] After a whirlwind three-month courtship, the couple was married on Christmas Day, 1871.

They had a good but often difficult relationship. Mary suffered from poor health during most of their thirteen-year marriage and resented the fact that Edison preferred working to coming home and spending time with her and their three children. Even though she suffered from many different ailments during her life, Mary's death on August 9, 1884, from "congestion of the brain" at the age of twenty-nine was a complete surprise.[30] Edison, who was not present when Mary died, was found the next morning at his wife's bedside "shaking with grief, weeping and sobbing."[31]

Edison, the consummate workaholic, didn't let his wife's passing slow him down. He continued working long hours and growing his many business ventures, usually with his daughter Dot by his side. Less than six months after Mary's death, at the World Industrial and Cotton Centennial Exhibition in New Orleans, he met another successful businessman, Lewis Miller, who was accompanied by his nineteen-year-old daughter, Mina. Edison was quite taken with Mina, even though she was engaged to the son of a preacher.[32]

There is some debate as to whether or not their meeting was completely by chance. Edison was already quite a famous inventor, and Miller may have been trying to set his daughter up with him. But whether it was pure happenstance or something Miller had been planning, thoughts of Mina distracted Edison from doing what he loved most—working. In Edison's diary, there's one recorded incident where he saw a woman that reminded him of Mina, and he became so enthralled by thoughts of seeing her again, he was almost hit by a streetcar because he wasn't paying attention to where he was going.[33]

In the spring of 1885, Edison went to Boston, where his friend and business associate Ezra Gilliland had a home. Boston also happened to be where Mina was attending a finishing school. While Edison was in town, the Gillilands brought many attractive women into their home for Edison to meet. One of them was Mina. No one knows how planned this meeting was, but whatever the circumstances, Edison was sold on Mina as a wife. Not only was she beautiful, but she could handle herself very well in the presence of the famous Thomas Edison. Most women who met Edison simply fawned over him.

Mina, who had grown up around rich and successful men, could hold her own. Edison found this quality extremely attractive.[34]

A long-distance courtship ensued. Edison went out of his way to meet Mina whenever possible. In September of 1885, just thirteen months after Mary's death, he sent a letter to Mina's father asking for permission to marry her. On February 24, 1886—seventeen months after the death of Mary—Edison and Mina were married in an elaborate wedding in New York City. At the time of their wedding, Mina was twenty years old—eighteen years younger than Edison and seven years older than Edison's oldest daughter, Dot. The couple had three children together and remained together until Edison's death on October 18, 1931.

***

In the latter half of the nineteenth century, the average life expectancy was around forty years. Being widowed at a young age wasn't as uncommon as it is today. Back then, it was the norm for most widows and widowers to remarry relatively quickly after the death of a spouse.

Aside from Dot, who found herself spending far less time with her father after he married Mina, there is no indication that any of Edison's family had concerns about him falling in love so soon after Mary's death or remarrying seventeen months after her passing. There is no indication that Mina or her family had any concerns about her marrying a widower with three young children. In fact, most of Mina's family was thrilled that she was marrying Edison instead of the preacher's son.

By all accounts, Edison had a good marriage with Mina. During their forty-five years together, there is no record that Mina felt like Edison loved Mary more or that she was competing with a ghost for Edison's heart. The only thing Mina ever had to compete with for Edison's time and attention were his various businesses.

Today, thanks to medicinal and technological advances, the average life expectancy is seventy-six years for men. Marriage rates are declining, and those who do end up tying the knot do so at a later age. As a result, being widowed at a young or middle age is more of a rarity than it was back in Edison's day. This results in a lot of confusion when it comes to the question of when to start dating again.

For example, many people have heard that the widowed should generally wait a year to start dating again, but these same people usually can't say why these rules exist or what the benefit is of following such advice. Unless a widower personally knows another widower who has gone through something similar, there are few reference points on how to navigate grieving, dating, and starting a new life with someone else. Modern portrayal of widowers in movies and novels are written by people with little knowledge of how these men actually grieve and move on. Widowers are generally shown as floundering through life until the right woman shows up, one who patiently waits until he's done grieving. Such pop culture portrayals is confusing for widowers and society at large, and they give no appropriate indication about to how to act and respond to men who are dating, or wanting to date, after their wife passes on.

To be fair, if it wasn't for my own experience, I probably wouldn't understand how it was possible for men to want to date again soon after their wife's death. I'd probably be highly critical of those who dated and remarried quickly.

My late wife, Krista, was raised by her widowed grandmother, Loretta. During the thirty years she was widowed, Loretta never dated or had any interest in a relationship. One day, one of her best friends died after a prolonged illness. The day of her friend's funeral, Krista and I were at her grandmother's home helping her get some food ready for the post-funeral gathering. While we were in the kitchen, her friend's widowed husband knocked on the door to pick something up. As he left, he turned and said to Loretta loud enough for all to hear, "I'll be calling on you later in the week." For what seemed like a very long minute, everyone was speechless.

Finally, Krista broke the silence. "Did he just ask you out?" she said, her mouth hanging somewhat open.

"I think so," Loretta said. "I hope I don't hurt his feelings when I tell him I have no interest in dating again."

We went back to our work without further discussion, but I remember thinking that the man must not have loved his wife very much if he was already thinking about dating before his late wife's body was in the ground. I imagined that the couple's marriage had been rocky for years and the widower was secretly happy his wife passed on. I thought the widower had some serious issues he needed to address before he even thought about dating. If Krista were to die, there was no way I'd be dating that soon. In fact, I couldn't see myself dating anyone again. I couldn't imagine myself with anyone but Krista.

About a year and a half after these events transpired, Krista took her own life and I became a young widower. The irony wasn't lost on me when, just two short months after her death, I noticed an attractive woman in the grocery store and, not seeing a ring on her finger, imagined myself asking her out. I felt guilty and confused for even having these thoughts. For several months, I was thoroughly confused as to how I should act and think. The few widows I did know were like Loretta—older women who never dated after their husbands' deaths and seemed content to live alone. I felt there was no one to whom I could turn for guidance and direction.

It turns out that my feelings were normal. In the last decade, I've talked to or emailed hundreds of young and middle-aged widowers and discovered that most of them had a similar desire to date again in the months following their wife's death. Only a handful of them actually asked a woman out, but the *desire* to date was strong. Now when I think back to that morning when the widower told Loretta of his feelings for her, I understand what he was feeling. (However, I still think he should have at least waited until sometime *after* the funeral before asking Loretta out.)

There is no set or correct timeframe for dating again. There's nothing wrong with you for wanting to date or start a new relationship weeks or months after your wife has passed on. Everyone reacts to the loss of a spouse differently. Though most widowers start dating within the first year, there are some who wait longer, and there are those who never date again. There is no right or wrong answer to this question. What's important is that before you take this step, you do everything possible to prepare yourself mentally to date again. (More on how to do this in the following chapters.)

Keep in mind that no matter how long you wait to start dating again, there will always be people who won't understand how you can be taking this step. They will think that you didn't love your late wife, had a rotten marriage, or may have been having an affair before your wife died. It's important that you not take anyone's negative reactions personally. Unless they or someone close to them has experienced the loss of a spouse, odds are they won't understand your desire to date again. But you should understand that your feelings are normal and there's nothing wrong with having them.

Even if the desire to date again is strong, just *thinking* about being with someone else can lead to feelings of guilt. If not understood and handled correctly, guilt can cause emotional turmoil, ruin any potential for a future relationship, and make your life a living hell.

CHAPTER 3
OVERCOMING FEELINGS OF GUILT

WHEN PIERCE BROSNAN was trying to make a name for himself as an actor in London, he met Cassandra Harris—a model and part-time actress who had a knack for making newspaper headlines. Despite the fact that Cassandra was twelve years older than Brosnan and had two children from a previous long-term relationship, the two immediately hit it off. After dating for a couple of years, they were married on December 27, 1980. Brosnan would later recall that marrying Cassandra was the best thing that ever happened to him.[35]

Cassandra turned out to be more than simply a good companion for Brosnan. She was a shrewd and ambitious woman who realized just how talented Brosnan really was. Despite the fact that she was only able to get small acting parts, she saw her husband as someone with the potential to be a world-renowned star and a man who could even play the role of James Bond in future films. (One of the bigger roles Cassandra managed to land over the years was Bond Girl Countess Lisl in *For Your Eyes Only*.) She also realized that if her husband were to achieve any of these dreams, they'd have to leave London and move to the United States. Eventually she convinced Brosnan to spend all their savings to move the family to Hollywood. It turned out to be a good move. Soon after they arrived, Brosnan got the lead role in the TV series *Remington Steele*, which kicked off a wildly successful acting career. For many years, life was great for Brosnan. He got good roles, had plenty of money, and his family life with Cassandra and three kids (including a son they had together) was stronger than ever. All that changed in 1987 when Cassandra was diagnosed with ovarian cancer.

For four years, Cassandra fought the disease. During that time, Brosnan put most of his professional commitments on hold, taking roles only when he thought his wife was well enough for him to be away. "When someone you love and cherish with all your heart has a life-threatening illness, nothing else matters," Brosnan said in an interview during her illness. "Whether I'm a successful actor isn't important anymore."[36]

Cassandra's fight with cancer had its ups and downs, and there were many times when they even thought she had beat it. Finally, her long struggle ended and she died in Brosnan's arms on the morning of December 28, 1991, the day after their eleventh wedding anniversary.

Brosnan was devastated. Despite having four years to prepare for this eventual reality, he had hoped for some sort of miracle. It took all his energy just to get out of bed in the morning. He vowed he would never marry again.[37] Even though he lost most of his ambition for acting, he kept at it here and there because that's what he thought Cassandra would want him to do.

At first, Brosnan struggled with the idea of dating again. When he finally started going out, he felt like he was betraying his late wife and their marriage.[38] "I was moving about with the greatest of ease and swiftness, not staying too long in any one place or with any one person," Brosnan said. "I had relationships. One feels guilt, but one needs to be held. It can be very difficult, because you feel you're betraying your past life and the wife you had."[39] One of the women he dated was Mateja Span, a Slovenian beauty Brosnan met while filming a movie in Yugoslavia. Despite their intense and immediate attraction to each other, Mateja said it felt like Brosnan's thoughts were never focused on her and that his mind kept drifting back to his late wife.[40] It wasn't until Brosnan met Keely Shaye Smith three years after Cassandra's death that he was able to put those feelings of guilt to the side for good. Keely gave Brosnan a new energy and zest for life. "Life goes on," Brosnan said soon after meeting her. "You cannot live in the past forever."

***

Most widowers feel like they're cheating on their wives when they start dating again. If these feelings bubble to the surface for you, don't feel like there's something wrong with you. It's a natural and normal reaction when you're still in love with your late wife and missing her sweet presence. Brosnan wasn't the only widower to have feelings of guilt once he started thinking about dating again. Joe Biden had similar feelings when he started thinking about relationships with other women. During a speech where Biden recounted losing his late wife, he said, "You're going to go through periods when, after a while, you'll see somebody you may have an interest in, and you're going to feel guilty as hell. You're going to feel this awful, awful, awful feeling of guilt" for thinking of another woman in that way.[41] The first time Paul McCartney saw Heather Mills, he felt bad for being so attracted to her. "Wait a minute, you're looking at other women," he said, recalling the first time he noticed her. "Immediately it was like, 'Uh-oh. You can't do that.' The married guilt. I beat myself up a bit about that."[42]

A couple months after my Krista died, I was at the

grocery store. As I swung the cart down an aisle, I nearly ran into an attractive blonde woman. Her hair color, features, and body type reminded me of Krista. I couldn't help but feel attracted to her. I wondered if she was single and would be open for a date. My fantasy lasted all of two seconds before it was followed by a strong wave of guilt. *What's wrong with you, Abel?* I thought. *Why are you even having those thoughts?* As I continued shopping, feelings that I was cheating on Krista overwhelmed me. I thought I was a terrible husband for even thinking such things. I had promised to love Krista forever, and just a few months after her death, I was already thinking about living a life with someone else.

By the time I arrived home with bags of food, I managed to brush off the guilt by telling myself that I would never think that way about another woman again. I rationalized that the thought had only popped into my head because the woman looked like Krista. I didn't really want to date or get to know that woman better; I just wanted Krista back in my life. At least that's what I told myself to get the guilt to subside.

Two days later, it happened again. This time I was stopped at a traffic light on my way to work. I happened to glance over at the car that pulled alongside mine. There was an attractive raven-haired woman in the car next to me. Even though she looked nothing like Krista, I found myself wondering if she was single. I assumed she was, and in a matter of seconds I imagined a life together. Just as the light turned green, she looked over at me, gave me a smile, and drove off. I pushed the thoughts of her from my head and spent the rest of the commute wondering what was wrong with me.

As natural as these initial feelings of guilt are for most widowers, they eventually fade away as you mentally adjust to the fact you're not married anymore and are free to date and have relationships with whomever you want. One of the best ways to get rid of these feelings of guilt is to go on a couple of dates with different women. The dates need not be long, complex outings. Something as simple as going out for a cup of coffee for an hour will help you make the necessary mental adjustments. During my first three or four dates as a widower, I felt like I was stepping out on Krista and meeting a mistress for a secret rendezvous. Needless to say, those dates didn't go well. However, each date did lessen the guilt somewhat, and eventually those feelings disappeared completely. By the time my future wife Julianna came into my life, I didn't feel any guilt about going out with her. As a result, I was able to fully open my heart to her.

After going out for a bit, if you find the feelings of guilt aren't going away, that may be a sign you're not ready to date yet. Give dating a break for a couple of months and try it again when you've had more time to adjust. Trust your gut. If you don't think it's the right time to date, don't do it. However, don't let feelings of guilt overwhelm you. There's nothing wrong with noticing other women and thinking about asking them out. You're not married anymore. Your thoughts and feelings are normal. The tricky thing is figuring out when you're mentally and emotionally ready to actually start dating again.

SURVIVOR'S GUILT

A second but less frequent kind of guilt arises after widowers find themselves in a serious committed relationship. Despite the fact that things are generally going well, the widower feels bad about being happy or falling in love again. Sometimes they feel like this because of the suffering the late wife experienced before she died. Other times, they don't feel they have the right to be happy when children, other family members, or friends are still grieving their late wife's death. Though not an official medical diagnosis, these kinds of feelings are colloquially called "survivor's guilt."

Survivor's guilt generally affects those who have endured some kind of traumatic event resulting in the death of others. It's also felt by people who experience traumatic, non-fatal events, like remaining employed when a coworker loses their job. Most widowers who have these feelings have usually lost their spouse to suicide or a prolonged illness. In most cases, they feel or wish they could have done more to prevent their spouse's death and now feel bad that they're enjoying life again.

To a degree, I can understand how these widowers feel. There were moments when I was dating Julianna and first married to her that I didn't think I deserved to be so happy or to be with such an amazing woman. I was generally able to shake off such feelings, but for the first year or two we were together, they would occasionally bubble to the surface. With the perspective of time, I can look back and see I felt this way because (1) I still had some residual guilt and feelings of responsibility for my late wife's suicide, and (2) I thought people who lost a loved one were supposed to be sad.

Overcoming survivor's guilt isn't an exact science. Everyone deals with it differently. However, if you've dated quite a bit or have started a serious relationship and still can't be happy with your new life, it could be a sign that you're not ready for a serious committed relationship. This doesn't mean you'll never be ready to take this step. Rather, you simply need more time to work though some issues. Instead of worrying about dating or a relationships, focus on doing things that will help you move forward. It's important for you to get to a point where you can feel happy about your blessings and the people already in your life—otherwise, feelings of guilt will destroy any romantic relationship you have. Until you figure out how to address it, having a functional long-term relationship will be impossible.

For me, overcoming survivor's guilt was all in my head. Whenever I felt I didn't deserve Julianna or have a smile on my face, I counted my blessings and realized there's nothing wrong with starting a new life, a new relationship, or just being happy. That may or may not work for you. However, I strongly believe that one of the reasons we're alive is to experience all the wonderful things life has to offer. We shouldn't feel bad when we find happiness or someone that makes us smile. Rather, we should be grateful for them and use our time, energy, and talents to make them happy too.

If you're experiencing something like survivor's guilt, realize that that most people are lucky to find true love once in their life. Not everyone can find it twice. Feel blessed and fortunate if you've been able to find someone else you can love just as deeply as the spouse you lost. Relish the happy times because, as those who have suffered loss know all too well, happiness and joy can be short and fleeting. There will always be unforeseen challenges that can quickly and unexpectedly turn one's life upside down. That's why it's important to be grateful for the good times and enjoy them. Let moments of joy and happiness envelop you. Take them in like you'll never experience anything like that again. Love is a great gift. Don't ever take it for granted or think something's wrong with finding it again. There are millions of others who would give anything to experience love, joy, and happiness right now.

Happiness is a choice. You can choose to feel bad about your new life and convince yourself that you don't deserve it, but the result of dwelling on loss and guilt is a long, miserable life. Never hold yourself back from experiencing people that can bring joy to your life. Life is too short to be miserable all the time.

Finally, when feelings of guilt do disappear, that doesn't mean you no longer love your late wife. It simply means you've reached a point where you can start making room for someone else in your heart. There is nothing wrong with that. It's normal and natural. Every day, countless widowers have relationships that are just as wonderful and fulfilling as their first marriages. That's something you can have as well—if you want it.

CHAPTER 4
GETTING YOUR DATING
LEGS BACK

FOR NEARLY THIRTY years, Paul McCartney was in a monogamous relationship with his wife, Linda. In the months following her death in 1998, McCartney was an emotional wreck. He wandered aimlessly around the house, talking about her, looking at the things she liked. [43] In the weeks following her death, friends and associates noted that he always seemed close to bursting into tears.[44] To cope with his loss, McCartney started doing everything in his power to memorialize his late wife. He released a posthumous collection of her songs, held memorial concerts in her honor, and his Blossom Farm home became a shrine to her memory.[45] McCartney also dropped out of the public spotlight. Aside from the occasional appearance at a memorial concert, he kept mainly to himself, shunning the press.

Then, thirteen months after Linda's death,

McCartney attended a charity event where he met a stunning blonde named Heather Mills. At thirty-one, Heather was twenty-five years younger than the famed Beatle, but her beauty and way with words had a mesmerizing effect on him. At first, he felt bad about desiring someone other than Linda. But his feelings of guilt were fleeting, and soon McCartney was convinced that Linda would be okay with him dating again.[46] Within days of their meeting, McCartney called Heather to talk about her charitable work. Soon the couple began a serious committed relationship. Being head over heels gave McCartney's life a purpose —something that had been missing since Linda died. With this newfound energy, McCartney began to write and record music again.[47]

Despite the feelings McCartney had for Heather, Linda always seemed to be part of everything the couple did. When Heather was first invited to spend time with McCartney at his home, she was put up at Blossom Farm—the same home that had become a shrine to Linda. Staying in that home with memories of Linda everywhere was too much for Heather, who ended up staying somewhere else nearby.[48]

The first time the couple was seen in public, it was for a choral concert to commemorate Linda's memory.[49] McCartney and Heather recorded an album together to benefit Heather's charity, something

McCartney had done many times for charities Linda supported. McCartney was even offered a commission to write a piece to dedicate the new auditorium at Magdalen College, Oxford. The college president suggested that a small, restrained piece would fit the academic nature of the university, but McCartney started thinking of something much bigger as a way memorialize his love for Linda.[50]

Heather also accompanied McCartney on a world-wide tour. Though McCartney would talk about Heather before playing "Your Loving Flame," many of his songs, including "My Love," commemorated his feelings for Linda.[51] So much of McCartney's life revolved around memorializing Linda that after a while, people could see Heather bristle every time Linda's name came up.

Despite the fact that Linda was always part of their relationship, Heather agreed to marry McCartney. The couple wed in a lavish ceremony in Ireland in June 2003, three years after they met. However, McCartney still wasn't able to let go of Linda. After Heather became pregnant with the couple's child, McCartney moved them into a home that was similar to the one he and Linda had enjoyed when they were first married. When they weren't out on tour, McCartney also asked Heather to cook for them every night—something Linda had done but something Heather resisted. Many speculated that McCartney trying to recreate the life he had enjoyed with first wife.[52] Heather, however, wanted none of it. Finally, after five contentious years, the marriage came to a very public and bitter end in 2008.

***

Most people viewed Heather as a woman who was interested in money, fame, and attaching herself to rich and famous men in order to meet her needs. And while Heather deserves much of the criticism directed at her, McCartney was not without his share of blame for the failed relationship. In fact, McCartney made four common mistakes that many widowers make when dating again. Had McCartney made some different choices, he might have avoided a disastrous relationship with Heather.

Mistake #1: McCartney Got Serious With the First Person He Dated

Even though he waited thirteen months after Linda's death before dating again, McCartney got serious with the first woman he asked out. No matter how much time has passed since their late wife's death, most widowers are in an emotionally vulnerable place when they start dating. Because most of them miss being married and the companionship that comes with it, they feel a strong desire to latch on to the

first person who shows a passing interest in †
The desire for someone in their life is so strong ᴜᴜᴜ
it can stop them from thinking clearly. As a result,
they can easily overlook warning signs and red flags
that the woman isn't a good fit for them or that she
might be using them—something that might be easily noticed if they were in a more emotionally stable
state. Heather is a beautiful woman and it isn't hard
to see why McCartney chose to pursue her. However,
after thirty years with Linda, McCartney dove too
quickly into a relationship before trying to figure out
where he was emotionally.

MISTAKE #2: MCCARTNEY RUSHED INTO A RELATIONSHIP

It's hard to blame McCartney for falling head over
heels for Heather. She was gorgeous, intelligent,
and had a way of getting men to notice her. After
being alone and grieving for thirteen months, having the company of such an attractive woman to
hold and talk to was undoubtedly very tempting.
But McCartney was so mesmerized by Heather that
he didn't take the time to get to know her before
getting dating her exclusively. One of McCartney's
good friends described the former Beatle as being
"cock happy" instead of being in love.[53] Blinded by
sex and the joy of having an attractive woman in his

life again, McCartney ignored any nagging doubts he may have had. It wasn't until after the couple had been married for several years and things were falling apart that McCartney acknowledged that he had ignored some red flags and that the relationship was indeed a mistake.

It doesn't matter if it's the first or one-hundredth person a widower dates—it's tempting for many widowers to rush into a relationship because it feels good to have company again. Companionship, however, isn't the same thing as a relationship. Getting serious with someone just because they're filling the hole in your heart will always lead to an empty and unfulfilling relationship in the end.

MISTAKE #3: MCCARTNEY COULDN'T LEAVE LINDA BEHIND

After Heather and McCartney got serious, there were always concerts and charity events and songs in Linda's memory. While some things may have been planned long before McCartney started dating Heather, such memorials continued all throughout the nine years the couple was together. There were always photos and other memories of Linda in McCartney's home, and he went as far as trying to recreate the atmosphere of his relationship with Linda after he was married to Heather. McCartney also wore the wedding ring Linda had given him until the day he married Heather.[54] Their relationship was never a relationship of two hearts, but of three—with Linda often occupying the biggest piece.

While there's nothing wrong with doing charity events or other activities that commemorate the late wife's memory, it becomes problematic when one is in a committed relationship with another woman. It takes a lot of work for any relationship to succeed. It's hard to hard to give your heart, time, and attention to someone else when you're still grieving or finding different ways to commemorate the past. Even things like looking at photographs of the late wife or keeping clothing that belonged to her can distract you from moving forward and starting a new life with someone else.

Mistake #4: McCartney Ignored Obvious Red Flags

Heather was engaged to documentary filmmaker Chris Terrill when she started dating McCartney. They even had a wedding date planned for later in the year. [55] When she went away with McCartney soon after they started dating, she lied to her fiancé and told him she was vacationing in Greece. When knowledge of her previous relationship came to light, McCartney brushed it off. Later, it became public knowledge that Heather had fabricated part of her past. She claimed she had made some money modeling in France when she had really been a high-end call girl for wealthy men.[56] She had also posed for a German pornographic magazine in the 1980s—which didn't seem to dampen McCartney's enthusiasm about the relationship in the least. The longer the couple was together, the more unsavory information about Mills was discovered. Yet when McCartney learned about unsavory aspects of Heather's past life, he simply brushed them to the side.

Everyone has a past and has done things they're not proud of or regretted later on. I'm a firm believer that people make mistakes, learn from them, and can change for the better. When getting to know someone, it's usually not fair to hold something against them that they did years or decades ago. However, Mills had a history of lying and using wealthy or famous men for her own needs. Had McCartney been thinking clearly, he might have realized that there were some issues that needed to be thought through before continuing his relationship with Heather.

***

For most widowers, it takes a little time to adjust to dating again. Since it's something they've haven't done in the years or decades since they became serious with their late wife, they're sorely out of practice. To complicate matters even more, they've become used to the habits and mannerisms of the late wife. Going out with someone who looks, talks, thinks, and acts differently from what they're used to can be like taking a trip to a country where you don't know the language or customs. That can lead to lots awkward or uncomfortable situations. The good news is that there are five things you can do to make getting back into the dating game easier.

TIP #1: MAKE THE FIRST FEW DATES SHORT

Don't make your first few dates long, formal affairs. Go out for a meal, a cup of coffee, or take a drive together. Just keep it short. I recommend this because many widowers are flooded with emotions and thoughts that don't make any sense when they're first dating. For example, it's common to feel that you're cheating on your wife or wondering if dating is even the right thing to be doing. By keeping the first few dates short and to the point, you can avoid being overwhelmed by these feelings. Having an hour or two with someone gives you plenty of time to analyze how you feel about the experience and whether or not it's something you want to do again. After you get a handful of dates under your belt and feel more comfortable doing it, then you can start going on longer outings.

My first date lasted all of two hours. It involved going out for lunch and talking for a bit after. The entire time I was flooded with memories and conflicting emotions. Looking back, two hours was just enough for the first time—at least for me. Even though the date wasn't great, it was perfect for getting my feet wet, and afterward I felt that it was something I wanted to do again. Two weeks later, I went out on my second date. It lasted about two hours as well. By my third date, I was feeling more confident. Soon I was able to handle dates that lasted all day.

Tip #2: Date Several Different Women

Because many widowers are hungry for companionship, it's easy for them to get emotionally attached to the first person they go out with. When they feel this way, it's hard to tell whether or not that person is really a good match for them. This can easily be avoided by dating several different people. This gives you a way to verify your feelings for the other person. If you feel like getting serious with every person you go out with, you're probably not ready for a serious long-term relationship right now.

Dating different people also gives you the chance to see how you stack up with a variety of personalities.

Over the years, I've received lots of emails from widowers who have become serious with the first woman they dated or the first person that showed some interest in them. In most cases, these widowers know there's something wrong with the relationship, but they can't quite figure out what it is. Eventually they realize that they started the relationship because they were lonely—not because they were ready to open their heart to someone else. And while there's no guarantee that any relationship will work, you can avoid pain, heartache, and wasting time simply by getting to know a lot of different women and evaluating your feelings when you're with them.

TIP #3: TRY NEW THINGS

When dating again, widowers tend to do things and go places they enjoyed with their late wives. It's easy to go to places that are familiar and where you know a good time will be had. But there are often strong memories of the late wife associated with these places, which can make the entire dating experience more difficult than it has to be.

One of the big concerns women have when dating widowers is reprising the role of the late wife. They often complain that they do a lot of the same activities with the widower that he and the late wife enjoyed instead of doing something that *they* want to do. Trying new activities and visiting new places can not only invigorate a relationship, but it makes it easier to move forward and decide if getting serious is something you're ready to do.

When I was first dating Julianna, sometimes we ate at restaurants or did other things that Krista and I had done together. I did it mostly because these were "safe" activities where I felt that things wouldn't go wrong. The last thing I wanted was a bad meal or something else to derail a relationship that, at times, was hanging by a thread. After we dated for a while, I started going to new places with her. Once I broke out of my shell and tried new things with Julianna, our relationship became much stronger. It also helped her feel that I was ready to start a new life.

Getting stuck in a routine is poison for any relationship. If you're out with a new person, try doing new things so you can have memories that are unique to your relationship. New memories and places never hurt anyone.

TIP #4: DON'T TALK ENDLESSLY ABOUT THE LATE WIFE

Would you enjoy spending time with a woman who went on and on about an ex? If not, how do you think women feel when they date widowers who can only talk about their late wife? While there's nothing wrong with covering the basics like how long you were married and when and how she died, it's best to keep early discussions focused on getting to know your date better instead of regaling her about your past love.

One of the biggest concerns women have when dating a widower is whether or not the widower is really ready to move on. Talking on and on about the late wife on the first couple of dates sends signals that you're not ready to start a new chapter in your life and makes the woman feel insecure. Your date's not there to listen to you talk about your past life in detail. She's doing the same thing you are—deciding whether or not you're worth spending more time with. Your date may be sympathetic and listen to everything you have to say because you're a widower, but don't mistake sympathetic listening for genuine interest.

I understand the need to talk about the late wife. When I started dating again, I wanted to talk and talk about Krista. I wanted to tell everyone I dated all about our marriage and what a great woman she was. Thankfully, one of the few things I did right was managing to refrain from doing that. Instead, I tried to focus as much as the conversation as possible on getting to know my date.

Don't misunderstand—I don't believe you should *never* talk about the late wife. If your date has questions beyond the basics, answer them. As you get to know her better and your relationship becomes more serious, there will be future opportunities where you can go into more detail. However, your first couple of dates aren't the right time or place for this. Dating isn't a therapy session—it's an opportunity to spend time with someone else and see what, if any, future the two of you may have together. If you find yourself dating just to talk about your loss, how much you miss your spouse, or tough times you're going though, your time and money would be better spent with a professional therapist. Besides, you and your date will have a more enjoyable and memorable time if it's about both of you instead than about everything you're going through.

Tip #5: Refrain From Playing the Widower Card

The absolute worst thing you can do when dating is to use your widower status to manipulate people or situations. Some widowers date a woman for weeks or months and act like everything's fine, but then they fall off the radar for days and weeks at a time without explaining they're not ready to date. Others blow off promises and commitments or treat their girlfriends poorly and use their grief as an excuse for their behavior. Some use their status to get money, sex, and sympathy from women for no other reason than to feed their egos or their personal needs without caring one bit for the feelings or needs of the women they're dating.

Don't ever do this.

If you find yourself using the loss of your wife to gain an advantage with the women you're with, you should not be dating. Give it a rest until you're ready to treat the women you date fairly and with respect. Pulling the widower card is classless and cruel. If you just want a relationship for sex without commitment or something else, man up and be honest about the kind of relationship you're looking for. It's not hard to find someone who can meet those needs.

I say this as someone who used the widower card in one relationship. Before I became serious with Julianna, I dated a girl I'll call Jennifer. I got into the relationship mostly because I was lonely and craved companionship. I wanted someone to talk to and be with, even if I had doubts about her or the long-term viability of our relationship. I was never honest with her about my feelings or what I wanted from her. I learned that if I behaved less than perfectly, as long as I blamed any bad behavior on my grief or loss, I could blow off promises or commitments or treat her badly without any consequences. For the three or four months we were together, I got everything I wanted out of the relationship. She got nothing.

What I did to Jennifer was wrong. Very, very, very wrong. I got a woman to think that she had found the love of her life, when in reality, there was never a chance that we were going to get married or have any kind of long-term future together. Then I dropped her like a hot potato once someone else came along. Don't be as cruel to the women you go out with as I was. Be honest and upfront about your doubts and feelings, no matter the consequences. If you do this, you'll move forward with your life faster.

CHAPTER 5
RELATIONSHIPS VS. COMPANIONSHIP

A FTER THE DEATH of his wife Cassandra, Pierce Brosnan became one of Hollywood's most desirable men. He was handsome, wealthy, and at the age of 41, still very much in the prime of his life. Women flocked to him. Brosnan started dating famous and attractive women, including the Julianne Phillips, the ex-wife of Bruce Springsteen, and Barbara Orbison, the widow of Roy Orbison.[57] Despite the seemingly endless supply of beautiful women who wanted to date him, none of the relationships lasted very long or became very serious. Brosnan still felt like half a person without Cassandra by his side and was content to drift from one relationship to another.[58]

All that changed, however, three years after Cassandra's death when Brosnan met Keely Shaye Smith on a trip to Mexico. From the moment he saw her, Brosnan realized there was something about her that made her different from all the other women he had been dating. Quickly, their relationship grew serious and she became a regular part of Brosnan's life. Unlike his other relationships, Brosnan didn't grow tired of her or feel like dating someone else. Instead, he found himself wanting to spend more time with her. Soon they were inseparable.

Smith renewed Brosnan's interest in acting. After only taking an occasional job after his wife died, Brosan began actively pursuing more work. Smith found herself accompanying Brosnan on trips overseas and to the premieres of his James Bond movies. His career, love life, and family life reached an apex when the couple tied the knot in August 2001.

Similarly, Joe Biden and Thomas Edison knew there was something special about the women they married after their wives died. The women they fell in love with brought more than physical attraction, someone to pass the time, or sexual fulfillment. Both men were unable to get thoughts of their future wives out of their minds. Edison thought of Mina so much when he was actively courting her that it became one of the few times in his life when he was unable to concentrate fully on his many businesses. He took every opportunity to visit her or write letters to her. It wasn't until after they wed and settled down that he was able to concentrate on his inventions and

work again—something he then attacked
renewed sense of energy and purpose.

Jill Jacobs gave Biden a purpose and direction that
had been missing from his life after Neilia died. He
embraced the Senate and the work it took to become
influential with other senators. With his renewed
energy and passion, he successfully ran for re-election and enjoyed the public spotlight. Years later,
Biden wrote how Jill had changed his life: "That's
when I realized exactly what Jill's love had done for
me; it had given me permission to be me again…
My whole life—for good and ill—I had been driven
by my passions, as if I needed to take the risk on all
the big things in life to feel alive. Jill made me see
that passion was still the controlling feature of my
existence."[59]

***

Whether they were married just a few short years or
many decades, most men have a hard time adjusting
to widowed life. They feel like a piece of them is
missing. To fix this problem, widowers try to find
someone to fill the hole in their life. Initially, most
widowers would prefer a life with someone—anyone—over being alone. Because of this, when widowers start dating again, they aren't necessarily looking for a relationship. Instead, they're looking for
companionship.

What's the difference between the two?

A relationship is based on love. It's when you want that person in your life because they're so amazing and wonderful that you can't imagine your life without them. Just thinking about them makes you want to be a better person. You'll honor your commitments and treat them like the center of your universe. You will move mountains and slay dragons for them. The relationship isn't about healing your broken heart (though that will happen), but about giving your heart freely to another and not expecting anything in return. It's about merging your life with the life of another and making something better and stronger that will last a lifetime.

Companionship is when you want someone to fill the hole in your heart. It's what you search for only because you miss having someone to talk to and to hold. You'll settle for just about anyone to make the pain and emptiness of being a widower go away. With companionship, you think only of yourself and your needs. The needs and happiness of the person you're with are of secondary importance—if it's a concern at all. Even when you know the relationship won't last, you can't let it go because life with someone you don't love is preferable to the alternative of a life alone.

As I mentioned in the last chapter, I got into a relationship with a woman named Jennifer for all the wrong reasons. I didn't intend for it to turn out that way. Jennifer and I had met years earlier. We never dated, but we were good friends. The relationship started when she called every week for the first month after Krista died just to check in and see how I was doing. At some point, I started calling her to chat. Though I don't remember what was said in those early calls, I do remember how good it felt to talk to someone about anything other than death and grieving.

Then our weekly phone calls became twice a week. Soon after that, we were talking on the phone nearly every day, and a long-distance relationship ensued. The conversations weren't anything special. Mostly she would talk about finishing her teaching degree and I would tell her about work and the house I was fixing up. Our phone calls became something I looked forward to. It was usually the only time during the day I felt I could have a real conversation with someone. Talking to her was more enjoyable than work-related conversations with coworkers or taut conversations with friends or family who, for the most part, still seemed to be walking on eggshells whenever I was around. I enjoyed the calls because, in some ways, they were similar to the day-to-day conversations I had with Krista.

Eventually, phone calls weren't enough. I flew down to Arizona to see her and she flew up to Utah to spend time with me. When we were with each other, Jennifer talked of a future together where I would either move to Arizona or she would come to Utah. At some point, marriage and kids became part of the conversation. Sometimes she spoke of growing old together. It was a vision that no matter how hard I tried, I was never able to share.

I liked Jennifer a lot, but never felt the same way as she did about the relationship. When I thought about the future, I couldn't see myself spending the rest of my life with her. I hadn't felt that way about Krista. When Krista and I were dating, the only thing I could think about was just how much I wanted to spend every moment of my life with her. Since I was a recent widower when dating Jennifer, I figured I had doubts because I was still grieving for Krista and eventually, my concerns about Jennifer and a future with her would go away. They never did. Instead, they became worse the more time we spent together. Despite my growing misgivings about my relationship with Jennifer, I continued it because I was afraid to be alone again. To me, that was a fate worse than being with someone I didn't love.

I had the opposite experience with Julianna. From the first time I saw her, I couldn't get her out of my head. Early in the relationship, we could spend all day together and I would go home alone at night feeling that it wasn't enough. Thoughts of her filled my mind, and when I wasn't with her, I counted down the minutes until we could be together again. I stopped thinking about my wants and needs, and I thought often about hers. Instead of expecting her to make me feel better, I worried about whether or not she felt the same way as I did about her. My zest for life returned. I started putting more effort in at work. I started reading books and writing again— two activities I was unable to do after Krista died. Julianna didn't do or say anything special to make me feel this way. She brought it out in me simply by being the person she was. As we spent more time together, I realized that the feelings I had for Julianna were the exact same feelings I had for Krista.

There's nothing wrong with dating because you're lonely. People mainly date because they want to find that someone with whom they can happily spend the rest of their lives. But there is a difference between pursuing a relationship for selfish reasons and self-less ones. Be honest with yourself and others about what you want out of dating. If you're just look-ing for a fun-filled short-term relationship or a one-night stand, say so. If you're looking for something more long-term and serious, let the women you date know that's what you want and then act like it when you're together.

Continuing the relationship with Jennifer sim-ply so I didn't have to be alone was wrong. As a result, I smashed the tender feelings and the heart of someone who had been a good friend and had done nothing to deserve the way I treated her. If I could do it all over again, I never would have let the relationship become as serious as it did. And I would have learned to deal better with my grief without using the feelings of someone else to help me cope.

And if you think a life with someone you don't really love is better than a life alone, consider this. In 1935, four years after Thomas Edison's death, his widow, Mina, married Edward Everett Hughes, a man who had been her childhood playmate in Ohio. The marriage was one of convenience. She called him "Mr. Hughes" and they slept in separate rooms. Sometime after their marriage, she told her personal secretary that "Dearie [Edison] was the only husband I ever had." [60] They remained together until Hughes's death on January 19, 1940. After his death, Mina again adopted the name "Mrs. Edison." Does that sound like a relationship you want?

CHAPTER 6
DATING WITH CHILDREN

B Y FAR, THE biggest question widowers face when they start dating is how and when to integrate a new relationship into the lives of their children. It doesn't matter if they're young kids, teenagers, or adults—merging a new life with an old one isn't easy. And there's no real way to know for sure whether or not your kids will accept the fact you're dating again or starting a serious relationship with someone until you actually start doing it.

There are, however, three things you can do to make this transition as painless as possible for everyone involved. As you read, keep in mind that the purpose of this chapter isn't to provide specific solutions for your particular situation. Rather, it's to get you thinking about things you do with your children to make it easier for you, them, and the woman you're dating.

***

Tip# 1: You Still Need to Be a Father and Parent to Your Children

After Joe Biden had dated Jill Jacobs for several months, he decided to introduce her to his young sons Beau and Hunter. Even though things were going well with Jill, he was nervous about whether the boys would accept Jill and how they would react to seeing him with someone other than their mother. Once he finally got Jill and the boys together, they all got along fabulously. From that point on, she became part of the lives of his two young sons. The four of them went on outings and extended holidays together.

After Biden and Jill had been dating about a year, Beau and Hunter came into Biden's bathroom where he was getting ready for the day. He could tell they had something important to say but didn't know how to broach the subject. Biden recalls the conversation this way:

> *Finally Hunter spoke up: "Beau thinks we should get married."*
>
> *"What do you mean, guys? Beau?"*
>
> *"Well," Beau said, "we think you should marry Jill. What do you think, Dad?"*
>
> *"I think that's a pretty good idea," I told them. I'll never forget how good I felt at that moment.*

"But, Dad," Beau said in all earnestness, "d'ya think she'll do it?"

They were observant, my sons. [61]

Even though the four of them were building a life together, Jill was still hesitant to marry Biden. One of her concerns was whether or not she could be a decent mother to two young boys. After Biden had proposed five times, Jill finally agreed to marriage. She spent the first few years of their marriage as a full-time mom to Beau and Hunter. She volunteered at the boys' school, made dinner, and drove them on annual summer trips to visit Neilia's parents. One day, Biden came home from work and noticed that boys were calling her "Mom" instead of "Jill." [62] It was a moment he never forgot.

Around this time, Beau and Hunter were asked by a reporter who was doing a story on the Biden family what they thought of their stepmom. Much to the reporter's surprise, the boys replied that they "didn't have a stepmom." [63] Confused, the reporter called Biden at his office for clarification. Biden and Jill were thrilled they had been able to successfully integrate their lives and make a family together. The boys' affection for Jill wasn't short-lived. Both Beau and Hunter continue to speak fondly of Jill and refer to her as their mom.

***

Part of the reason Biden had an easy time getting his boys to accept Jill was because he did everything in his power to give them a stable environment after their mother died. With the help of his sister, Val, Biden gave them a home where they could be watched over by someone they were already familiar with. Despite their loss and the injuries they suffered in the wreck, Beau and Hunter were still expected to follow the house rules, do chores, go to school, say their prayers, and be on their best behavior.[64] It wasn't an easy transition, and Biden's work schedule and long commute were not ideal. However, Biden and his sister were able to give his boys a place where they could feel safe and a routine they were expected to follow. Having these things in place gave the boys a firm foundation. So when Jill came into their lives, her presence wasn't adding confusion to existing chaos.

All kids need structure and stability when living at home, but it's especially important to provide this after they lose a parent. That means whatever house rules and expectations were in place *before* their mother died should still be in place now. They need to know that even though they've lost someone near and dear to them, some things—including your love for them—are going to remain the same. Too often, widowers fall into the trap of easing up on the rules because they feel bad for what their kids are going through. While some adjustments may need to be made, kids can get spoiled or become accustomed to getting their own way because they know their mother's death has lowered what's expected of them.

Bad behavior is bad behavior. Don't let you children get away with things because they're sad or grieving. If you let "Mom's death" become an excuse for acting out, getting bad grades, or staying out past curfew, you're going to quickly end up with a disrespectful child. Your first duty to your kids is to continue to be a parent to them. And if there's ever a time when they need a father in their life, it's after their mom has passed on.

Have them help around the house and do other chores to keep themselves busy. Widowed parents often feel that they have to do everything themselves. That's an impossible burden for anyone to bear. How much the kids should help out depends on their age and ability. Whether it's setting the table, cooking dinner a couple of times a week, mowing the lawn, or cleaning the bathrooms, they need to shoulder some of the responsibility to keep the house running as smoothly as possible.

This also applies to adult children who are no longer living at home. Even though they may not be living with you anymore, making excuses for their bad behavior when they're with you and the woman you're dating is unacceptable. You should expect the same behavior from them when they visit your home as you did before their loss.

Being a widowed father, especially if you still have kids living at home, is hard work. Pierce Brosnan found it to be an overwhelming responsibility and described it this way: "It's very demanding and you feel very alone and scared about making decisions you used to make with your partner, whether it be simple decisions like what you're going to have for dinner or how to sort out finances and issues about schooling. Suddenly you're Mum and you're Dad." [65]

In addition, there may be issues that *you* need to work through. It may seem like you never have a moment to process or think about what happened because of the needs and wants of your children. The duties and responsibilities that come with your new role can seem crushing. But despite the enormity of the charge before you, it's vital that you don't stop being a parent and a father to your children, no matter how old they are.

If you don't think any of this is important or necessary, let me share a story that Jenn, a reader of my blog, left in a comment in order to illustrate what can happen when you abdicate your responsibilities.

> *I am the child of a widow (my father died when I was 8), and my mother was guilty of overindulging us. It was awful. I felt guilty every time she gave us anything because I knew she was*

doing it in an attempt to compensate for the loss of my father. It didn't work—there isn't anything that can make up for a loss so significant. Indulging a child on occasion is okay—doing it as a way of parenting on a regular basis is not. My brother was younger when my father died, so he pretty much grew up with an attitude of expecting to get everything he wanted, whenever he wanted it. He is still this way.

What kids need when a parent dies is consistency, understanding, and for the remaining parent to actually BE a parent, not a friend. Whatever rules were in place BEFORE the mother died should be in place now. I understand being more flexible at first—when your whole world has been turned upside down. But you cannot live, and you definitely cannot thrive, in the upside-down world. Kids need to know that even though there has been an ENORMOUS change that some things are still unchanged. I would have felt safer if my mom had still been the same mom (regarding her rules and expectations of me) after my father's death as she was before.

I know that it can't be easy (my mother definitely struggled) to say "no" to a child who has lost a parent, but they need it. Otherwise, it's like losing two parents. As a kid who was overindulged after losing her father, all I can tell you is that what

I wanted was for my mother to be my mother. I NEEDED restrictions, I NEEDED proper nutrition, I NEEDED a bedtime, and I NEEDED to hear no. All kids do. Would I have whined and been upset at times? I'm sure I would have, but all kids do—it's a normal part of growing up. I ended up parenting myself for the remainder of my childhood, and while it definitely made me more mature, I admit that I still feel resentment toward my mother for her "softness" after my father died. [66]

Even though your role in your children's lives evolves as they get older, move out of the house, and have families of their own, a father is something you'll be for them not matter how old they are. That comes with a huge set of responsibilities. Don't shrink your duties simply because of a life-changing event. If there is a time when your children need you the most, it's after they've lost their mother.

***

After Thomas Edison's first wife, Mary, died, Edison found himself a father to three young children. Raising kids wasn't exactly Edison's forte. However, he did allow his 12-year-old daughter, whom he affection-ately nicknamed Dot, to accompany him to at work, on business trips, and in his lab. He even got her into smoke-filled "men's restaurants" after work where women were usually not allowed. [67] There she would eat ice cream, buy her father nickel cigars, and listen to her father and his friends talk about business. Since he was a workaholic, this was the first time in her life that she was able to spend large amounts of time with him. After several months of this treatment, Dot was convinced she was her father's favorite child. [68]

However, the most memorable and happiest part of Dot's childhood came to an abrupt end once Edison married Mina. Once he tied the knot, Edison's old habits returned. He threw himself back into his various business ventures, and the one-on-one time Dot spent with her father was reduced to almost nothing. Dot referred to the year after her father's marriage as "the most unhappy of my life," as her father spent most of his time with his new wife and work. [69] Dot yearned for the days when she never left her father's side, but those times were never to return. Dot blamed Mina for ruining her childhood and taking her father away from her. She often referred to Mina as her "second mother" and said she could never take the place of her real mom.[70]

As she got older, the relationship between Dot, her father, and her stepmother became more strained. The relationship between Dot and her father was so bad that at one point, they went seventeen years without seeing each other.[71] Eventually, Dot came to have an amicable relationship with her stepmother and father, but it was a process that took decades. Part of her would always resent the fact that she had to share her father's time and attention with a woman who was just seven years older than herself.

TIP# 2: KEEP THE LINES OF COMMUNICATION OPEN

Thomas Edison did a lousy job of integrating his new wife into the lives of his three children. All of them were young when they lost their mother, which, to some extent, should have made this task easier. However, Edison didn't want to be burdened with being a father or the duties of parenthood. After marrying Mina, he expected his kids to fall in line and accept their stepmother.

Edison's tendency to put work above all else—including the needs of his wife and children—created an environment where his kids felt like second or third place in his life. For Dot, the feelings of abandonment were even more intense. After spending lots of time with him after her mother died, she was immediately relegated to her old place when Mina became her stepmother.

Once a widower gets in a serious relationship, it's common for his children to feel like they're losing their dad. They may feel that they're being replaced by the new woman he's dating or that he's closing the door on the memories of the old family.

In addition, you might be ready to date and move forward, but your kids may still be grieving the loss of their mother. They may not understand how their father can be moving on while they're still sad and struggling with their loss. Some kids may also worry that the woman you're dating is looking to steal their inheritance or not have your best interests at heart. No matter the reason for their feelings, they'll often do everything in their power to drive a wedge between you and the woman you're dating. Behavior can range from being openly rude to her, giving her the silent treatment, or talking bad about her when she's not around to defend herself. Other times, they try to sabotage activities you have planned by coming up with last-minute emergencies.

You can save everyone a lot of heartache and avoid misunderstandings by talking and communicating with your children in a safe, private environment. Give them a place where they can vent, talk, and express how they really feel—not only about you dating again, but about how they're dealing with the loss of their mother and anything else that is on their minds. The purpose of this isn't to solve their problems or tell them they're wrong, but so you can better understand where they're coming from. In addition, it gives you a chance to tell them why you're dating again, how you've moved forward in the grieving process, and why you've decided to become serious with someone else. If your kids don't feel like they can have these conversations with you, they may refuse to participate. But it's something you need to try and establish, not only for the sake of any future relationship you may have, but it's good practice for other family issues that will inevitably arise.

Don't confuse this activity with getting their permission to date. You can't let your kids control your life, no matter how old or young they are. The purpose of this is to give everyone chance to understand how others are feeling. It's also a way to let them know that you still love them and their mother. With this information, you can figure out the best way to balance dating and any new relationship with your children's needs and integrate anyone you get serious with into your old life.

TIP# 3: LISTEN TO YOUR KIDS, FAMILY, AND FRIENDS

On New Year's Eve in 1996, six months after meeting Heather Mills, Paul McCartney finally introduced her to his kids—an event that was awkward and difficult for everyone.[72] The fact that McCartney and Mills were a couple was already known to his children, as the relationship had been splashed around the British tabloids for months. However, McCartney had been hesitant to make any formal introductions until then.

Heather had already met most of McCartney's close friends and associates, and none of them liked her. Many were still grieving the loss of Linda and viewed Mills as a phony who was dating the former Beatle for his money or a way to boost her own visibility and career. After the meeting on New Year's Eve, McCartney took his three kids on a holiday trip to a resort in the British West Indies. Heather didn't join them. Instead, she waited a few days, then flew in after all of McCartney's children had left for home.[73]

The relationship between Heather and McCartney's children never got any better as time went on. They all expressed their opinions to their father about Heather, but he ignored what they had to say. When McCartney married Heather four years later, only two of McCartney's daughters, Mary and Stella, attended the wedding. His adopted daughter, Heather, and son, James, stayed home, as they were strongly against their father's marriage. As his marriage to Heather began to unravel, Stella allegedly said to her father, "I told you she was a bitch. Why did you marry her? She's been a manipulative cow from day one. The cow won't be happy until she destroys all of us and our memories of our mother."[74] James later admitted that his relationship with his stepmother wasn't very good. All of McCartney's children were glad when his marriage to Heather ended.

Three years after his divorce from Heather Mills

was finalized, McCartney married Nancy Shevell—a woman twenty-five years his junior. This time, all of McCartney's children embraced their father's new wife. When asked about Nancy, James said, "Nancy's my new mother. I feel that. Definitely. She's very genuine. I knew her a year or so before she married Dad. She has been one of the biggest supporters of me doing this, pursuing my own dreams. She wants me to have my own career. She makes Dad very, very happy. We all adore her." [75]

***

No matter how much you want things to work out between your children and the woman you're dating, you can't force them to like each other. There are many factors, such the age of your kids, how long it's been since their mother died, and the quality of your communication with your children, that affect how accepting they are of each other. However, that doesn't mean you should simply ignore what your children and others have to say.

What's notable with Heather Mills is that not one of McCartney's close friends or of his children liked her. Those who were close enough to McCartney and expressed their honest opinion were ignored. McCartney lived in a world where everyone told him how great and wonderful he was. Despite his age, he went on world tours and played to sold-out stadiums. Surely a man like that couldn't make a mistake when it came to matters of the heart.

The truth is, sometimes widowers don't think straight when they get serious with someone. (I talk more about this in Chapter 4.) It never hurts to get a gut check from friends and family members you trust to make sure the woman you're dating really is a good fit for you and your family. This is especially important if you have minor children living at home, since this woman may have a hand in raising them.

When I was dating Jennifer, none of the friends and family I introduced her to liked her. They didn't have to say anything for me to get the message. I could tell simply by the way they acted around her. They weren't rude to her and they didn't treat her badly, but I could tell they weren't embracing her, either. Inside, I was upset that they didn't like her as much as Krista. However, I figured that since it had been less than a year since Krista died, they were still grieving and were simply having a hard time seeing me with someone else. Looking back, I think their grief played a relatively small role in their actions. Most of it had to do with the fact that they didn't think she was a good fit for me. Many of them told me as much after the relationship ended. When these same friends and family met Julianna a few months later, the reaction from just about everyone was the opposite. They genuinely liked her and thought she was wonderful. They didn't have to tell me that either. I could tell by the way they acted around her that they hoped the two of us would have a long and successful relationship.

Like McCartney, I had a hard time seeing that Jennifer wasn't a good fit for me. (With the gift of hindsight, I can see that marrying Jennifer would have been a complete disaster and wouldn't have lasted long.) Friends and family could see that it wasn't right. I wish someone had said something to me about Jennifer. At the time, there were two or three people I actually might have listened to. It's hard to know whether or not this would have shortened my relationship with Jennifer, but it would have been nice to be told I should take a step back and look at the bigger picture.

If your children express concerns about the woman you're dating, *listen* to them and try to figure out the real reason for their concern. Pat responses like "I don't like her" don't cut it. Drill down and figure out what their concern really is. Maybe they're still grieving the loss of their mother and aren't ready to see you with someone else. Maybe they're worried about being cut out of your will. Maybe they're worried you'll forget about them and stop spending time with them. But maybe, just maybe, they see something that you can't see because of all the strong, crazy emotions that come with losing the love of your life and opening your heart to someone else. It doesn't hurt to take some time to reflect on the relationship and decide why you're really moving forward with it. It's possible some of their concerns will reflect some deep, internal doubts you have about the relationship. Sometimes it takes a third party to help you see whether you're thinking with your head, your heart, or another part of your body. Doing so can help you avoid a relationship that could turn into a long-term disaster.

Though their opinions are important, you don't need the permission of your friends and family to date or to get into a committed relationship with someone else. And when you ask for people's opinions or when they give them to you unsolicited, you need to take them with a grain of salt, as not everyone has your best interest at heart.

There also aren't any magic words you can say to get your kids to accept your new relationship or to successfully integrate a new woman into their lives. Every family and situation is unique. However, by giving them a caring home environment, a place where they feel safe expressing their feelings, and getting a gut check from friends and family members you trust, you can go a long way toward making sure that the transition from your old life goes as smoothly as possible.

CHAPTER 7
THINK OUTSIDE THE LATE WIFE

SOMETHING THAT THE second wives of Joe Biden, Pierce Brosnan, Thomas Edison, and Paul McCartney all had in common is that they were very different from the late wives in looks, interests, and personality. For example, Thomas Edison's first wife, Mary, was blonde, gray-eyed, full-figured, and sociable,[76] while Mina was dark, petite, and on the quiet side.[77] But their differences went far beyond their looks.

Mary was a sixteen-year-old employee at Edison's telegraph tape company and was the daughter of a sawyer—someone who cut wood for a living. After she married Edison, she never forgot her working-class background. She remained a favorite among her former fellow employees, who considered her to be one of their own.[78] In some ways, her marriage to Edison was difficult for her. Edison was a workaholic and would often sleep in his lab or office instead of his own bed. As a result, Mary often felt neglected, and as the marriage wore on, she became insecure, withdrawn, and desperate to please her husband.[79] With Edison rarely at home, she often relied on her older sister and parents for company and emotional support. In addition, she suffered from health problems that made it difficult to maintain the Edison household and be a mother to their three children.

Edison's second wife, Mina, was more up to the challenge of being the spouse of a famous businessman. Her own father was wealthy and also ran many successful businesses. She was a high school graduate, attended a finishing school, and had traveled throughout Europe. She was used to being around the rich and famous, and after they were married, she readily adapted to Edison's erratic work schedule and needs. She dubbed herself a "home executive" and supervised a staff of maids, gardeners, and cooks.[80] She also handled Edison's social calendar and did most of his public relations so Edison could spend time doing what he did best—inventing and running his many business ventures.[81] She was exactly the kind of woman Edison needed at that time in his life.

***

When widowers start dating again, most of them instinctively start looking for someone like the late wife. They often pursue women who have similar looks or have related interests and personalities. There's nothing wrong with doing this per se. It's normal and natural to pursue someone who has attributes or interests we're already comfortable with—especially after we've spent years or decades with someone comparable. The problem is that when dating women who are akin to the late wife, widowers often expect the new woman to *behave* like the late wife. They quickly learn that these women have their own lives, personalities, and interests, and the widower often will end things when the relationship wasn't what he expected.

When I started dating the second time, I met most of the women I dated via an online dating site. I had my search set up so it would only show women who were creative and artistic or had the same interests as Krista. Despite the fact that many of them were like Krista on paper, I was inevitably disappointed at the end of the dates because they were nothing like my late wife. I thought that as long as the women I dated had a personality or interest I was familiar and comfortable with, I'd have a better chance of connecting with them on a romantic level. Jennifer not only looked like Krista, but had a very similar personality. However, I was never able to click with her in the same way I did with Krista. Much to my surprise, it turned out that I connected with

Julianna—someone who was the polar opposite of Krista in terms of interests and personality.

What I've learned in the ensuing years is that Krista and Julianna are strikingly similar in many ways. However, I had to look deeper into them to discover what it was that made me want to marry them. I'm going to suggest that instead, you think about seven different areas of compatibility that take a deeper dive into what really made you compatible with the late wife. I came up with these areas one day while wondering how I could fall in love with Krista and Julianna—two people who seemed, at least on the outside, to be the exact opposite of each other. When I came up with this list, Julianna and I had been married for several years and out of the blue, I realized that both of these women shared some common core values and beliefs.

Since then, I've talked to widows and widowers who have had successful second marriages, and most of them agree that their late spouses and their second spouses matched up well in these areas. Sometimes the second wives matched up better than the previous spouse because the widower had a better idea of what he could or could not live with the second time around.

I don't claim that this list is everything you need to think about in order to decide if someone you're dating is worth spending the rest of your life with.

It's an opportunity to decide what's really important to you at this time in your life. My personal opinion is that you need to match up in at least six of the seven areas in order for the relationship to have long-term potential. But that's just my opinion. Building a life together is more than just compatibly. It's also all about communication, compromise, knowing what you can or cannot live with before you get serious with someone, and not settling for someone who isn't everything you want in a partner.

One final thought: When reading through the seven points below, if the other person doesn't match up, don't assume they're going to change if you love them more. Odds are, they're going to be the same person tomorrow that they are today. What you need to decide is if you can live with their differences.

AREA #1: PHYSICAL ATTRACTIVENESS

You should be physically attracted to the person you're dating. This may seem like a no-brainer, but sometimes widowers will settle for women they aren't attracted to just to have a relationship with someone. I made this mistake with Jennifer. Don't be as dumb as I was.

Physical attraction helps kick-start the relationship and sustains it later when you get more comfortable with each other. Even though Jennifer had familiar characteristics, I was never physically attracted to her the way I was to Krista, or later to Julianna.

While there's nothing wrong with dating someone who looks like the late wife, keep in mind that you run the risk of expecting her to act like someone she's not. Widowers who do this run the risk of bringing back memories of the past instead of thinking about the future. It can also make the woman you are dating hesitant to get serious with you, as she might feel that she's simply a replacement instead of your real love.

Don't settle for someone who doesn't excite your heart and turn you on when you look at her. Doing so will just create another roadblock in finding the relationship you really want. If you're attracted to the person now, you'll be attracted to them tomorrow and decades from now when you're both old and gray.

AREA #2: PERSONAL VALUES

Everyone has religious, moral, spiritual, or other philosophical values that guide their lives. These values play an important role in what one thinks and how one behaves. You need to decide how important it is for someone you're dating to have the same or similar values as yourself. Think back to your relationship with your late wife. Were similar or different values and beliefs a source of conflict or harmony in your marriage? Is this something you would change the second time around?

When considering someone's values, you need to think about more than religious or philosophical issues. How do you feel about drinking, smoking, white lies, drug use, pornography, and gambling? Did you or your late wife have any of these problems? If the woman you're dating had one or more of these issues, could you accept it or would you have a hard time living with it again? Could you be honest with someone you're dating about any of the aforementioned issues that you currently have or had dealt with in the past?

It's extremely important to me that my wife and I have similar beliefs and values. I'd have a hard time living with someone if she felt differently about certain things. For you, being similar in this area may not be a big deal. You need to decide just how important this is for you and what you can and can't live with.

AREA #3: RECREATIONAL ACTIVITIES

What kind of activities do you enjoy in your free time? Are there things you like to do alone, or do you prefer to have someone enjoy them with you? Would you want anyone you get serious with to enjoy the same activities, or at least support your participation in them?

Recreational activities aren't something you have to enjoy with that special person in your life, but if they're time-consuming, you may need their support in order to participate in them. For example, Julianna likes to run marathons. If you've never run one, doing all the required training for a 26.2-mile race is very time consuming. Even though I don't run marathons, I'm fully supportive of this activity. I'm more than happy to watch the kids for several hours on Saturday mornings so Julianna can do her long runs, or even put all the kids in the minivan and meet her every three miles or so along her training route in order to give her something to drink and a bit of encouragement.

Similarly, Julianna knows I love to write. Even though she has no interest in writing herself, she understands that I need sixty to ninety minutes most days to work on books, blog posts, and other things. And she goes out of her way to make sure I have it. (She's lying in bed next to me reading a book as I write this.)

Whether you participate in the same activities isn't nearly as important as whether or not the two of you can support each other in the things you like to do. Some people have a hard time if their partner's activities take them away from them or their family for extended periods of time.

Think back to your marriage to the late wife. Did she support you in your recreational activities? Did you support her? Or were other activities a source of conflict in your marriage? Decide what you can live with and seek out someone who can either do the activity with you or at least support you in doing it.

AREA #4: MONEY AND FINANCES

Money, or lack thereof, is one of the main causes of stress in many relationships. It's also one of the leading causes of divorce and breakups. This isn't a topic you need to bring up on the first date, but it's something you should talk about as your relationship gets more serious.

Think about how you live when it comes to debt, paying bills, investments, savings, college funds, living month-to-month, and personal spending money. Does the woman you're dating feel the same way, or does she have a different view of finances? How much money must you have annually in order to feel that your needs have been met? Does the woman you're dating feel the same way? Are there any financial problems that you would or would not be willing to live with? Are you okay with separate checking accounts, or do you need to share one?

When it comes to finances, Julianna and I are in lockstep agreement. We avoid debt and live within our means. It's something we talked about quite a bit when we were getting serious because I knew I couldn't live with someone who viewed money and finances differently.

The fact that we have the same views about money has saved us lots of stress. There have been times when money's been tight and we've struggled to make ends meet. But because we're on the same page as far as spending, budgeting, and debt goes, we've been able to work together and get through the tight financial times with minimal marital stress. If financial stress is something you'd like to minimize, make sure that you and the woman you're dating are close to being on the same page, or that you can reach some happy middle ground.

Krista wasn't a big saver or budgeter, but she did avoid debt and helped ensure that we weren't living beyond our means. There's always room for compromise, of course, but if one person likes to spend money like there's no tomorrow while the other person is more financially responsible, there will be a lot of stress and fights in your future—especially if money gets tight.

AREA #5: SEX

Sexual compatibility can be an issue for some widowers. They may have difficulty becoming intimate because they're grieving the loss of their spouse and feel guilty about getting close to someone else. Other times, their guilt and grief can lead to performance issues.

Whenever you feel ready to become intimate with someone else, it's important that you're emotionally ready to do it and not just looking to fulfill your physical desires. Learning how to enjoy it with someone who has different needs and desires than your late wife can take patience and practice.

How important is it for you to be with someone who shares your sexual interests, beliefs, and desires? Do you need to be with someone who can openly discuss sexual matters? Would you have a problem with the woman you're dating looking at pornography or masturbating? How often do you need to have sex? Would it cause a problem if you weren't able to have sex as often as you desired? What sexual problems or performance issues would you be willing to live with?

If you're waiting until marriage to be intimate, does the person you're dating share the same values? Can the two of you talk about sexual needs and wants before you're married? Are you willing to be patient with each other while you learn how best to please the other person after you tie the knot?

Sexual intimacy is something that can strengthen a relationship if both partners are in agreement as to the right time to become intimate and the purpose of intimacy in their relationship. The best way to figure this out is to be open and honest about what you expect in the bedroom and then work with the other person to meet those needs.

AREA #6: EDUCATION, INTELLIGENCE, AND WORK ETHIC

Most people want to be with someone who is on a similar level with them intellectually. However, one's education does not necessarily translate to intelligence. Just because someone has a Ph.D. doesn't mean that they have the ability to carry on a coherent conversation with you. Conversely, someone without a college education isn't an idiot. But it generally helps if you can find someone who can at least be up to your level in the brain department.

This also doesn't mean that you have interests in similar subjects. Krista, like me, had a liberal arts degree. Julianna, on the other hand, has a chemistry degree. Despite these differences in interests, they both met my intellectual and conversational needs. Whether you have similar or diverse intellectual interests, what's important is that you find someone you feel you can talk to. So as you date, ask yourself what kind of intelligence and/or education do you need a spouse to have in order to respect her. Does she have what you need for an intellectually fulfilling relationship?

Along a similar vein, is the person's work ethic and what they do for a living important? Does it matter to you what her career is? Is it important to you that she's financially successful? If she lost her job, would you be okay living on less? Is it important to have her home a lot, or would you mind if she worked late? How would business trips and long hours affect your relationship?

There's nothing worse than being with someone who bores you to death or doesn't live up to your work expectations. It helps to find someone who can meet whatever intellectual expectations you have. It makes your relationship stronger when both of you meet each other's mental as well as emotional needs.

Area #7: Family

We discussed the perils and pitfalls of dating with children earlier in the book, but I'm going to take this section a bit farther. Everyone has slightly different views of family. For example, some questions to ask yourself include the following: Do you need to be with someone who will put you first, before other family members or their dependent children? What roles do you need your spouse to assume to have a happy relationship? What step-parenting issues or problems are you willing to face? Is it important that the woman you date likes your kids and is open to you spending a lot of time with them? Do you want more children? If so, how many? Does your spouse feel the same way?

This was the one area where Krista and I were different. We never matched up in the role we wanted our extended families to play in our lives, or in how many kids we wanted. As a result, 95% of the stress and arguments in our marriage came from family-related issues. When I started dating again, I promised myself I wouldn't marry someone who didn't share my beliefs about family life. Thankfully, Julianna and I match perfectly. As a result, we have fewer fights and less stress in our marriage.

***

Everyone is different. There are no right or wrong answers to the questions posed in these seven areas. What's important is that you find someone who is a good fit for you. If you feel that the woman you're dating is compatible in six out of the seven areas, odds are the two of you have enough in common to make your relationship work. If you got less than six out of the seven, take a step back and ask yourself why you're in the relationship and whether or not you can really spend the rest of your life with this person.

No one is going to be exactly like your late wife. No matter how many women you date or how similar they seem on the outside, they're all unique and different. Every one of them is going to have things you love about them and things that drive you crazy. What you need to decide is *why* you're attracted to the person in the first place. Is it because she's an amazing person in her own right, or because she reminds you enough of the late wife that it eases your grief and the pain in your heart? If it's the latter, you're bound to be disappointed as you get to know her better. Don't be afraid to date outside your comfort zone. It never hurts to go on one date with someone who may seem to be the polar opposite of the late wife.

Dating the second time is quite an adventure. Don't be afraid to see all the different options out there. You might be surprised at what you find.

CHAPTER 8
10 CONCERNS WOMEN HAVE WHEN DATING A WIDOWER

DATING A WIDOWER isn't easy. Most widowers don't understand just how difficult it is. The women who date them, however, learn very quickly that dating a widower is nothing like dating a divorced or single guy. Women who date widowers have to deal with a host of unique relationship issues, and they have little support and struggle to find someone to turn to when questions or concerns arise.

When I was first dating Julianna, I felt that I was ready to move forward and start a new life with her. Julianna didn't see it that way—at least when we were first dating. She had some major concerns about becoming serious with someone who had recently lost a spouse. There were several times when our relationship nearly ended because she thought I wasn't fully ready to give my heart to her, or she had her own doubts about spending the rest of her life with someone who would always have a special place in his heart for another woman.

I share this because when you start dating again, there may be some women who refuse to date widowers or who abruptly end the relationship, even if you think things are going well, because there are some issues they simply don't know how to or don't want to deal with. Others will have major misgivings about getting into a serious committed relationship with someone who has lost a spouse—especially if that person's loss is recent.

It's important that you don't take these rejections or concerns personally. Unless they've lost a spouse, it can hard for others to understand why you're even dating again. However, this doesn't mean you should shrug off their concerns or think they aren't important. If you're dating with the goal of having a committed relationship, it's better that you understand the worries and apprehensions women have about dating or being in a committed relationship with a widower so you're better able to see their side of things and understand why they're asking certain questions, saying certain things, or behaving in certain ways.

Below, you'll find the top ten concerns women have when dating a widower. You can help the women you date overcome some of the issues.

Others, however, are something the women have to figure out for themselves. Remember that most women aren't going have *all* of these concerns. Some may have just one or two, while others might have more. Their worries depend on their own relationship history, how you behave when they're with you, and whether or not you're ready to start a new chapter in your life.

Concern #1: Why Are You Dating Again?

The more recently you've been widowed, the bigger an issue the time since you're wife's death becomes. Women are going to be more worried about dating someone who's been widowed six months as opposed to six years. No one wants to be the rebound relationship—the one who's only there to fill the hole in your heart, fulfill your sexual needs, or be someone for you just talk to. They want to feel like more than just a mom for your kids or a replacement for your late wife. They want to be loved, valued, and appreciated for who they are.

Very few of the women you date will express this concern directly. Instead, they'll ask questions like how long you've been widowed or how long you've been dating. If you're under a year, the first thing they're going to wonder is why you're dating again so soon, even if they don't come out and say it.

You can help resolve this issue by knowing why you're dating again and being honest and upfront with any potential dates about why you've taken this step. Say you've been widowed nine months. When the subject comes up, it might be helpful to say something like, "You're probably wondering why I'm dating so soon," and then be honest as to why. If you feel you're ready to move on, say so. If you're looking for something short-term without any attachments or commitments, be honest about your intentions. If it's something you're just trying out to see how it feels, that's okay too. The real issue isn't why you're dating, but whether you can be honest with yourself and others about it. If you can't tell someone about where you are emotionally and why you've taken this step, you're probably not ready to date. Don't worry about someone refusing to go out with you because of your honesty. If the date has any chance of blossoming into the kind of relationship you desire, you've got to be honest with them from the very beginning. Relationships built on a foundation of dishonesty will eventually crumble to the ground.

Concern #2: Will You Ever Love Me As Much As Your Late Wife?

After someone dies, they tend to become saints in the minds of those who knew them. All their faults—no matter how bad—are overlooked or forgotten about, while all the wonderful things they did are what people tend to remember. When the woman you go out with hears stories about your late wife, they're usually about what a wonderful wife, mother, daughter, and friend she was. Odds are she's not going to hear about the time the late wife yelled at you or the kids or did something shortsighted and stupid.

In addition to hearing all the great stories about her, if the women you date visit your home, they're going to see the late wife's pictures on the wall and her things in the bedroom or on her shelves. They're going to see bits and pieces of a relationship that meant the world to you, but no longer exists. It's easy for anyone to wonder if you're ever going to be able to make room in your heart for someone else.

The only real way to convince someone you love them is through your actions. You need to *show* the women you go out with that you're actually ready to open your heart to them. Instead of talking about your loss and the past all the time, get to know *her* likes, wants, and needs.

Make your home a place where the woman you're

dating can feel comfortable. Pack up or give away things that tie you to the past and hold you back from starting a new life chapter. Move mountains, slay dragons, and go to the ends of the earth just to make her smile. Do it not because you feel obligated, but because you want to do things that will make her happy.

No one is asking you to forget about the late wife or to stop loving her. Those who ask you to wash away your past completely aren't ready to date a widower. These women have to understand that there will always be a special place in your heart for your late wife. However, there's nothing wrong with her asking you to have 99.9% of your thoughts and attention on her. The best way to alleviate any concerns she has is to *show* her that you're ready to make her number one.

CONCERN #3: I CAN'T TELL HIM HOW I REALLY FEEL

For some women dating a widower can be like constantly walking on eggshells because they don't know what they can or can't talk about in regards to your late wife, your past, or your future. If they say what's on their mind, will you think of them as insensitive or mean? Others worry that talking about certain subjects will bring back memories of the late wife and make you start grieving again.

For example, I've heard stories from women who felt they couldn't bring up a trip to California because that's where the widower and the late wife went on their vacations. Some women who work as nurses feel like they can't talk about their day out of fear that it will trigger a tidal wave of memories and emotions of the widower's wife passing away in a hospital.

In the year following my late wife's death, I could tell there were times when friends and family didn't know what to say when I was around, or they would start talking about certain subjects and then stop because they were unsure what would set me off. I hated every minute of it. I don't blame friends, family, and the women I dated for acting the way they did or dancing around certain subjects. Had I been in their position, I would have behaved in a similar manner. However, all I really wanted was to be treated like a normal person and to have normal conversations. Looking back, I wish I had done a better job of alleviating their concerns. For example, when the subject of suicide, guns, or babies came up, I should have told them they didn't have to tiptoe around certain things.

Don't be afraid to let others know that they can act like themselves if you're around. If there's a subject that's still raw and hard to talk about, that's fine—just let them know you can't go there at this time, but might be able to at some point in the future. The women you date will appreciate your honesty and feel more comfortable talking to you. It's best to learn how to communicate with each other sooner rather than later, and this will solve a lot of problems before they have a chance to mushroom and destroy a relationship.

CONCERN #4: WHAT IF HIS KIDS DON'T LIKE ME?

It doesn't matter if you have young kids, adult children, or something in between—it's hard to be in any relationship if your kids are throwing fits. Many a relationship with a widower has come to an end because the widower's children made life a living hell for the woman.

Chapter 6 in this book is devoted to dating with kids, which I encourage you to read if you haven't already. But in short, you should expect your kids, no matter their age, to treat any woman you introduce them to with the same respect they would have given their mom. Yes, kids have wants and needs that should be addressed, but you need to make sure that they haven't learned to use their loss to treat people badly. While most women will understand that kids have a mind and thoughts of their own, you can go a long way in overcoming this concern by having a backbone and standing up to misbehaving kids. Relationships between kids and a stepmother-type figure will generally improve over time. They'll get worse if you allow things to spin out of control from the beginning instead of manning up and being a dad.

Concern #5: Will His Relationship With the Late Wife's Family Interfere With Our Relationship?

This concern usually arises after you're in a serious, committed relationship. Most women don't care if you still have a relationship with the late wife's family, especially if you have children living at home. This concern tends to bubble to the surface when the widower ends up spending more time, holidays, or other special occasions with the late wife's family instead of the woman he's in a serious relationship with. It makes the woman you're with feel that you'd prefer to live in the past and aren't ready to make her the center of your universe.

Prioritizing existing relationships while understanding that you can't make everyone happy is one of the challenges widowers face when dating again. At some point, you're going to have to adjust some long-standing relationships as you get serious with someone else. When and how they change is ultimately up to you. But any romantic relationship won't work if there are more than two hearts involved. It doesn't matter if the third heart is your feelings for the late wife, her family, your friends, or your job. In the end, what you say doesn't matter. How much time you spend with someone shows where your real priorities are.

I never had very strong ties to most of my late wife's family, and though I did introduce Julianna to most of them, they were never a big part of my life after Krista's death. However, I did have close ties to many friends. I spent a lot of time with one couple who were best friends with Krista and me. Once I was in a committed relationship with Julianna, I had to cut back on the amount of time we spent together. It wasn't because my friends and Julianna didn't get along, but I realized that in order to strengthen my relationship with Julianna, I needed to spend more time with her.

Prioritizing relationships can be one of the more difficult decisions widowers have to make because there's always going to be someone who's not happy with the results. Then again, some of the most difficult choices can be the most rewarding if we make the right ones. Don't be afraid to spend some time thinking and pondering about the best way to handle these delicate situations. Depending on your relationship with the late wife's family, it might be a good idea to introduce them to the woman you're dating once you're in a committed relationship. They might get along just fine and enjoy spending time together. And if they don't, that's okay too. Whatever happens, you've got to man up and figure out what relationships are truly important and move forward.

Concern #6: When Will He Stop Grieving?

Most widowers are still grieving to some extent when they start dating again. There's nothing wrong with that so long as the widower is ready and willing to do what it takes to open his heart to someone else instead of using his dates as therapy sessions. After all, no one wants to waste their time with someone who's going to be sad or difficult to live with.

Unless the woman has lost a spouse, she probably doesn't know how long it takes for most people to get over it. But she will be watching your actions, or lack thereof, to decide if you're really ready to take this step.

Here are a few things that make women think you're not ready for a new relationship:

Sharing pictures and stories of you and your late wife on Facebook or other social media sites. I can't begin to explain just how much this makes women think you're not ready for a serious relationship. Think before you post or comment. Is this something you really want everyone—including any women you're dating—to see? Are the comments or pictures something that will strengthen your current relationship or harm it?

Regular visits to the cemetery. No one is going to begrudge you an occasional visit to the late wife's grave. However, if you're going more than a couple of times a year, it makes the women you're dating wonder where your heart really lies, especially if you come home sad or in a mood. Think about how these visits make you feel. Do they hold you back to the past or do they help you move forward?

Constantly talking about the late wife and your past life. You have a past and should feel comfortable sharing stories from your old life. However, there's a time and a place for everything. If every conversation returns to the subject of your late wife or what the two of you did together, there's a problem. How would you feel if the woman you're dating constantly talked about her ex-husband or boyfriend? The women you date feel the same way.

The best way to resolve the above concerns (or others I haven't mentioned) is through your actions. If you behave like you're moving on, or at least showing that you're making progress in opening your heart to someone else, it is less of a concern.

Most experts will tell you that it takes twelve to eighteen months after the death of a spouse to work through grief. What they don't say, however, is that when you meet the right woman—one you can see yourself spending the rest of your life with—it doesn't matter how much time has passed since your late wife died. You'll figure out a way to work through any unresolved issues because you can't imagine not spending every day with this person, not just because you feel like you're supposed to. That's what happens when you meet someone you really want to have a committed relationship with.

If you're giving it your best effort but you find that your grief isn't getting better or you feel that you're stuck in the same place emotionally, stop dating for a bit and give yourself time to work things out. You might even want to see if there's some professional who can help you move forward. You shouldn't be in a committed long-term relationship—or even dating again—if you aren't making progress. It's not fair to you or the woman you're dating to continue a relationship when you're not fully ready to take that step

Concern #7: Will He Want to Make New Memories with Me?

No one wants to feel like they're helping you relive the past. Relationships are more enjoyable and exciting when the couple is actively making new memories and sharing new experiences. Yet often, women who date widowers feel like they're reliving the widower's previous marriage.

As they learn more about you, the late wife, and the relationship the two of you shared, they may see that you're stuck in the same routines from your previous marriage. This isn't good for you, your ability to start a new chapter in your life, or the long-term viability of your relationship.

The good news is that this concern can easily be undone no matter how old you are or how long you were married to the late wife. If you go to new places and try new activities together, it will be like a breath of fresh air in your relationship. If you're unsure what to do or how to get started, learn everything you can about the woman you're dating and figure out what activities she likes. Don't be afraid to try something new, or think that you're too old to break out of your routine. Just the making the effort of trying new and different things can go a long way toward showing her that you're serious about moving forward.

Concern #8: Will He Give Up His Widower Status?

Let's be honest—widowers get a lot of sympathy and attention. As we discussed earlier in the book, being a widower can serve as an easy excuse for all sorts of lies and bad behavior. It also comes with other advantages that some widowers find difficult to give up. Unless the woman you're dating has previous experience dating a widower, it can take some time for this concern to manifest itself. But even before she realizes it's a concern, widowers know whether or not their status is something they're willing to give up for the right person. And if you're not willing to give up the understanding and special privileges that come with your loss, you shouldn't be dating. Period.

Putting your wants and needs above the person you're dating is poison to any relationship. Dating with the intent to start a new chapter in your life requires you to man up. That means you need to stop thinking of yourself as a widower and taking the excuses people give you because of your loss. Instead of thinking about what others can do for you, put the desires of others ahead of your own. It's not a difficult thing to do when you meet the right person.

There's a big mental change that needs to happen in order for anyone to move forward and start a new life. If you can't make this mental shift, you'll never truly fall in love with someone again. That's fine if you want to be alone. It's not fair, however, to the women you date to let them think that you're ready to change for them when, in your heart, you have no intention of doing that.

Concern #9: How Long Will the Photographs, Facebook Pages, and Other Memorials Stay Up?

Once your relationship reaches the point where you feel comfortable bringing the woman home to meet your kids or just to spend some time together, one of the first things they're going to notice is the photographs and other mementoes that memorialize your marriage and life with the late wife. As your relationship gets more serious and nothing in the house changes, they're going to wonder if you're really ready to move on.

Many of the photographs and other things in your house probably haven't changed much and you might not even notice them. Take a minute and look around your home and ask yourself if it's a place you'd feel comfortable visiting if you were in her shoes.

Most widowers don't realize how hard it is for a woman to come to your house and see all the memories and reminders of the past. Women understand that you've lost someone and will put up with the pictures and other visible memories for a short time, but at some point, it hinders your relationship because they don't see anything that shows you've embraced her as part of your new life. At some point, she will bring it up by asking where the pictures of the two of you are, or telling you how those reminders affect her. When this subject does arise, it's important not to take her concerns personally or think that she wants you to forget the past. All she's really asking is that you show that you love her too and that you make your home a place where she can feel comfortable.

I was more aware of this concern than most people. The home I was living in when I was dating Julianna was one I fixed up after Krista died. I put every photograph on the wall myself. When my relationship with Julianna reached a point where she was spending time at my home on a regular basis, I could tell the few pictures of Krista bothered her. Even though she never said anything to me about them, I noticed that her eyes would linger on some of the photos, and there were times when she looked uncomfortable. Once I started taking down photos in places like the living room and kitchen where we spent most of our time, I found that Julianna was willing to come over more often. Eventually, I took all the photographs down and packed them up so she would feel comfortable in any room in our home.

Finally, don't forget that pictures and memorials on Facebook and other social media accounts can make the women you date think you're not ready to move on. One can avoid the photos in the home by simply not going there. However, often the women you date are flooded with photos and trips down memory lane when they log in to a social media account—whether they want it or not. Posting a past vacation picture and sharing great memories of the past may be fun and generate lots of comments and likes from friends and family, but most women view it as a sign you're more in love with the past than with them.

How many photos (if any) to leave up in your home or post on social media is something you're going to have to figure out for yourself. (And you should feel free to let any children who are still living at home have whatever memories of their mom they want in their bedrooms.) Just remember that photos and other objects have the ability to trigger memories and feelings that can slow your progress and make it difficult to move forward.

Concern #10: I Don't Know How to Act on Certain Days

When dating a widower, there are certain anniversaries that non-widowed couples don't have to deal with. The day the late wife died, their wedding anniversary, and her birthday are the top three that come to mind. Even regular holidays like Christmas, New Year's Day, and Thanksgiving can be somber affairs because the late wife isn't there to celebrate with the rest of the family.

As difficult as the date-of-death anniversary can be for widowers, it can be equally as complicated and awkward for the women they're dating. There's no manual on how to behave on these days. In addition, what widowers choose to do on these days can vary from special religious celebrations to an outing to the cemetery or nothing at all. To make matters worse, widowers can get sad, moody, or depressed on the days leading up to one of these anniversaries, and their moods and emotions can last for days or weeks after. When you factor in that your time and attention are focused on someone you still love, but who is no longer living, there's enough stress, worry, and confusion to drive even the strongest women crazy.

The good news is that dealing with this concern is simple—communicate what, if anything, you're going to do on those days and any role you would like the woman you're dating to play in these events. If you want to go to the cemetery or previously scheduled events alone or just need time to yourself, that's fine, so long as you're upfront and honest with her about what you're doing and what, if anything, is expected of her. For example, if you're going to the cemetery on the anniversary of her death, tell the woman you're dating what you're doing, how long it's going to last, and, if you want, invite her to come. If you'd rather spend the day alone or with your kids, friends, or other family members, tell her it's nothing personal, but you just need some time apart for a day. It may not be easy to do, but it will work out better in the long run if you can establish a pattern of honesty and communication. If you don't, the woman you're dating will wonder how you're really feeling, and it can quickly turn into a bigger issue than it needs to be.

Finally, if you invite her and she doesn't accept, don't take it personally. There are thousands of reasons why she could decline. Whatever the reason, don't get upset or discouraged at the news. Go have your day and then come home and do what you can to make the woman you're dating feel like a queen.

Dating a widower can be one of the most emotionally intense and confusing relationships a woman ever experiences. Though you can't solve every concern, there's a lot you can to keep the stress and confusion to a minimum. Most of it can be done by learning how to communicate with her and then showing her that she is the center of your universe. Every relationship is going to have its own unique set of issues. The sooner you both learn to talk, compromise, and work things out, the better chance your relationship has of lasting the rest of your lives.

CHAPTER 9
FALLING IN LOVE AGAIN

THROUGHOUT THIS BOOK, I've written a lot about getting your dating legs back and given you some tips and tricks for making the transition to this phase of your life as easy as possible. But there's one last issue I want to address. It's for those widowers who are dating because they're looking for someone they can spend the rest of their lives with. The ones who want another relationship that's just as fulfilling and wonderful as the one they had with the late wife. It's something I'm asked often by widowers who are dating and still trying—and sometimes struggling—to figure things out. How does one know that they've fallen in love enough with someone to spend the rest of their lives with them?

This question comes up because there's a gaping hole in a widower's heart after the death of a spouse. It makes it easy to confuse the excitement of companionship with love. After all the sorrow, pain, and anguish widowers have gone through, it usually feels good to have someone in their lives again, regardless of whether or not they're a good fit.

Because we've been so low emotionally, it's easy to settle for someone who is simply willing to spend time with us and put up with the emotional wrecks we can be. Often, we start serious relationships that, under normal circumstances, we never would have been part of otherwise.

Thankfully, knowing when we've fallen in love the second time around isn't that hard to figure out. When you fall in love, I mean *really* fall in love, you'll feel the exactly the same about this new woman as you did for your deceased wife. Think back to the days when you first fell in love with your late wife and knew she was the person you were going to spend the rest of your life with. Remember those feelings and emotions that were coursing through your body at that time and then compare them to the feelings you have now. Most men knew there was something special about their late wife when they first met, even if they weren't sure exactly what that was. It's that strange, special connection two people have. It's something that Thomas Edison felt when he met Mina. Joe Biden felt it the first time he laid his eyes on Jill. Pierce Brosnan felt it when he was introduced to Keely. It happened to me the first time I noticed Julianna.

Now think about the woman you're dating or per-haps want to date. Does she make your heart pound in your chest in that boom, boom, boom sort of way? Does the sadness and sorrow in your life fade away when you're with her or think about her? Do you feel like you've known each other forever? When you're not with her, do thoughts of her consume you to the point of distraction? Does she make your life feel like it has more meaning and purpose than it's had in a long time? Does she make you excited and invigorated about living again?

The first time I saw Julianna, it felt like electricity was coursing through my body. It was a feeling I'd never felt before or since. It happened despite the fact that I didn't know who she was or anything about her. Yet that feeling was so intense, I knew there was something special about her. I needed to understand why a complete stranger could evoke such a reaction. After our first date, all my feelings about her were confirmed. They were still there the second time we went out. By our third date, there was no doubt in my mind that she was someone I could happily spend the rest of my life with. Nine months after we started dating, we tied the knot. We've been married eleven years. I've never been happier.

Maybe you'll experience something like that the first time you see someone. Maybe you won't. There is, however, a thrill that comes when we click with someone. But that feeling of excitement doesn't always last. Sometimes the feeling fades away in a couple of weeks or months. Generally those relationships don't last long. But when you find one of those special people you can spend the rest of your life with, that feeling of excitement never goes away. It's always there somewhere to remind you just how much she means to you.

When we meet the right person, we're willing to love them for the person they are—faults, good traits, and everything in between. There are no nagging doubts or questions about whether we're ready to start a new chapter with her because we *want* to spend the rest of our lives with her. We're willing to sacrifice our old life and start a new one. It's a journey that should sound familiar to widowers because it's something you did once before. At some point, you left your single world behind and started a new one with your late wife. It's a journey you'll want to take again when you meet the right person. It's a journey I hope you're willing to take when the opportunity presents itself.

OTHER BOOKS BY ABEL KEOGH

Relationship Guides

*Dating a Widower: Starting a Relationship
with a Man Who's Starting Over*

*Marrying a Widower: What you Need
to Know Before Tying the Knot*

*Life with a Widower: Overcoming Unique
Challenges and Creating a Fulfilling Relationship*

Novels

The Third

Memoir

Room for Two

ACKNOWLEDGEMENTS

A big shout out to the widowers who gave feedback on this book as it was going through the various drafts. Also to the women in the Dating a Widower Facebook group who gave their insight on certain chapters. Finally, many thanks to Tristi Pinkston and Amanda Rowan their editing and proofreading suggestions.

But the biggest thank you goes to Julianna for giving me the time to write another relationship guide. None of my books are possible without your love and support. You're my best friend and I love you most times eternity.

ABOUT THE AUTHOR

At the age of twenty-six, Abel Keogh unexpectedly found himself a young widower. When he decided to starting dating again he looked in vain for resources that could help him guide him through the dating waters and open his heart to someone else. Finding nothing, he stumbled through dating, fell in love with Julianna, and convince her to marry him. As of this publication they've been married for eleven years and hope to live to a ripe old age and spend the rest of their lives together.

Abel and Julianna live somewhere in the great and beautiful state of Utah. As members of the Beehive State, he and his wife Julianna are the parents of the requisite six children.

Learn more at http://www.abelkeogh.com.

REFERENCES

Introduction

1 Danielle S. Schneider, Paul A. Sledge,
    Stephen R. Shuchter, and Sidney Zisook.
    "Dating and Remarriage Over the First
    Two Years of Widowhood," *Annals of
    Clinical Psychiatry* 8, no. 2 (1996): 51–57,
    doi:10.3109/10401239609148802.
2 Jane E. Brody, "Getting on With Life
    After a Partner Dies," *New York Times*,
    June 14, 2010, http://www.nytimes.
    com/2010/06/15/health/15brod.
    html?_r=0.

Chapter 1

3 Elisabeth Bumiller "Biden Campaigning With
    Ease After Hardships", *New York Times*,
    December 14, 2007, http://www.nytimes.

com/2007/12/14/us/politics/14biden.
html

4 Joe Biden, *Promises to Keep: On Life and Politics* (New York: Random House, 2008), 80.

5 Ibid., 80.

6 Ibid., 81.

7 Ibid., 80.

8 Beau Biden, Transcript of Remarks delivered to the Democratic National Convention, *Politico,* August 27, 2008, http://www.politico.com/news/stories/0808/12913.html.

9 Biden, *Promises to Keep*, 80.

10 Ibid., 86.

11 Ibid., 88.

12 Ibid., 93.

13 Ibid., 100.

14 Ibid., 101.

15 Ibid., 101.

16 Ibid., 118.

17 Ibid., 116.

18 Transcript of Joseph R. Biden Jr.'s Speech at the Democratic National Convention, *New York Times,* August 27, 2008, http://elections.nytimes.com/2008/president/conventions/videos/transcripts/20080827_BIDEN_SPEECH.html.

19 Biden, *Promises to Keep*, 88.

20 Ibid., 89.

21 Ibid., 89.

22 Ibid., 89.

23 Ibid., 88.

24 Ibid., 93.

25 Ibid., 96.

26 Ibid., 96.

Chapter 2

27 Neil Baldwin, *Edison: Inventing the Century* (New York: Hyperion, 1995), 52.

28 Mike Connell, "Thomas Edison Fell Out of Love with Port Huron" *The Times Herald*, November 6m 2011, http://www.thetimesherald.com/article/20111106/OPINION02/111060314/Mike-Connell-Thomas-Edison-fell-out-love-Port-Huron.

29 Baldwin, *Edison: Inventing the Century*, 53.

30 Ibid., 143.

31 Ibid., 143.

32 Ibid., p 147–148

33 John D. Venable, "Mina Miller Edison: Daughter, Wife and Mother of Inventors," Edison Muckers (blog), http://www.edisonmuckers.org/daughter-wife-and-mother-of-inventors/

34 Ibid.

Chapter 3

35 Peter Carrick, *Pierce Brosnan* (New York: Citadel Press), 41.

36 Ibid., 66,

37 Jane Warren, " Pierce Brosnan: The Tragic Death of My Wife Helped Me Prepare for My Latest Role," *Express*, April 6, 2013, http://www.express.co.uk/news/show-biz/389712/Pierce-Brosnan-The-tragic-death-of-my-wife-helped-me-prepare-for-my-latest-role.

38 Lawrence Grobel, "Pierce Brosnan: More than just a Beautiful Bond!" *Cosmopolitan,* September 1, 1996. Reprinted at http://piercebrosnan.jamesbond-online.com/pbarticle_MoreThanJustABeautifulBond.html

39 Matthew Wright. "Passionate Pierce in Oh-Oh Heaven; Bond Star Reveals His Licence to Thrill", *The Mirror.* August 23, 1996. Reprinted at http://www.thefreelibrary.com/PASSIONATE+PIERCE+IN+OH-OH+HEAVEN%3B+Bond+star+reveals+his+licence+to...-a061312175

40 Carrick, *Pierce Brosnan*, 114.

41 David A. Fahrenthold, "Biden Shares Tales

of Loss with Families, Friends of Military Casualties," *The Washington Post*, May 25, 2012, http://articles.washingtonpost.com/2012-05-25/politics/35458119_1_vice-president-biden-delaware-democrat-military-families.

Chapter 4

42 Anthony DeCurtis, "Paul McCartney on 'Beatles 1,' Losing Linda and Being in New York on September 11th", Rolling Stone, June 17, 2011, http://www.rollingstone.com/music/news/paul-mccartney-on-beatles-1-losing-linda-and-being-in-new-york-on-september-11th-20110617.

43 Howard Sounes, *Fab: An Intimate Life of Paul McCartney* (Philadelphia: Da Capo Press, 2010), 482.

44 Ibid., 484.

45 Ibid., 496.

46 Ibid., 490.

47 Anthony DeCurtis, "Paul McCartney on 'Beatles 1,'," ,

48 Howard Sounes, *Fab: An Intimate Life of Paul McCartney*, 496.

49 Ibid., 495.

50 Ibid., 503.

51 Ibid., 512.

52 Ibid., 524.

53 Ibid., 500.

54 Caroline Gammell and Gordon Rayne, "Heather Mills and Sir Paul McCartney: Timeline of the Relationship," *The Telegraph*, 18 Mar 2008, http://www.telegraph.co.uk/news/uknews/1582052/Heather-Mills-and-Sir-Paul-McCartney-Timeline-of-the-relationship.html.

55 Howard Sounes, *Fab: An Intimate Life of Paul McCartney*, 495.

56 Ibid., 499.

57 Peter Carrick, *Pierce Brosnan*, 113–114.

58 Ibid., 185.

59 Joe Biden, *Promises to Keep*, 118.

60 Neil Baldwin, *Edison: Inventing the Century*, 413.

Chapter 6

61 Joe Biden, *Promises to Keep*, 115.

62 Ibid., 119.

63 Ibid., 120.

64 Ibid., 88–89.

65 Julie Carpenter, "Family Tragedy Returns to Haunt Pierce Brosnan as his Darling Daughter Dies of Cancer," *Express*, July 3, 2013, http://www.express.co.uk/news/showbiz/412083/

Family-tragedy-returns-to-haunt-Pierce-
Brosnan-as-his-darling-daughter-dies-of-
cancer.

66 Jenn, comment on "Widower Wednesday: Man Up and Be a Dad," October 17, 2012, http://www.abelkeogh.com/blog/widower/widower-wednesday/man-up-and-be-a-dad/.

67 Baldwin, *Edison: Inventing the Century*, 114.

68 Ibid., 145.

69 Ibid., 171,

70 Ibid., 257.

71 Ibid., 314.

72 Ibid., 497.

73 Ibid., 497.

74 Anthony Barnes, "At Last, What Stella McCartney Really Thinks of her Step-mother," *The Independent*, October 29, 2006, http://www.independent.co.uk/news/uk/this-britain/at-last-what-stella-mccartney-really-thinks-of-her-step-mother-422088.html.

75 Caroline Graham, "My Rift with Dad, Lost Drug Years and the Night Mum Died, by James McCartney: Paul's Son Gives His First Ever In-depth Interview at 35," *Mail Online*, June 13, 2013, http://www.dailymail.co.uk/news/article-2342148/

My-rift-dad-lost-drug-years-night-mum-died-JAMES-MCCARTNEY-The-depth-interview-son-Paul-McCartney.html#ixzz2iji95pgB.

Chapter 7

76 Baldwin, *Edison: Inventing the Century*, 53.

77 Ibid., 147.

78 " Mary Stilwell Edison," National Park Service website, http://www.nps.gov/edis/historyculture/mary-stillwell-edison.htm.

79 Baldwin, *Edison: Inventing the Century*, 61.

80 "Mina Miller Edison," National Park Service website, http://www.nps.gov/edis/historyculture/mina-miller-edison.htm.

81 "Mina Miller Edison: A Valuable Partner to Thomas Edison," *Edison Muckers*(blog), http://www.edisonmuckers.org/mina-miller-edison/.